# JERUSALEM

By Colin Thubron
and the Editors of Time-Life Books

Photographs by Jay Maisel

THE GREAT CITIES · TIME-LIFE BOOKS · AMSTERDAM

**The Author:** Colin Thubron was born in London in 1939, descendant of the first English Poet Laureate, John Dryden. After leaving Eton in 1957, he worked in publishing, then travelled extensively in the Middle East and the Orient, where he made several documentary films for television. His first book, *Mirror to Damascus*, is a study of Syria. He has since written *The Hills of Adonis* (after a four-month walking tour of The Lebanon), *Jerusalem* (an earlier work on the city), and *Journey into Cyprus*. He is also the author of a novel, *The God in the Mountain*, and is a Fellow of the Royal Society of Literature.

**The Photographer:** Jay Maisel was born in Brooklyn, New York, in 1931. He studied painting at Cooper Union Art School and at Yale University, where he abandoned art for a career in photography. His pictures have appeared in numerous magazines and books, including several volumes published by TIME-LIFE BOOKS. He has also had many one-man exhibitions of his work. To get the pictures for this book, he made two trips to Jerusalem, one in autumn, one in winter.

*EDITOR*: Dale Brown
*Picture Editor*: Pamela Marke
*Design Consultant*: Louis Klein
*Staff Writer*: Deborah Thompson
*Researchers*: Gunn Brinson, Vanessa Kramer,
Jackie Matthews, Jasmine Spencer
*Designer*: Graham Davis
*Assistant Designer*: Roy Williams
*Design Assistant*: Shirin Patel
*Picture Assistants*: Cathy Doxat-Pratt,
Christine Hinze, Marilyn Miller

The captions and text of the picture essays were written by
the staff of TIME-LIFE BOOKS.

Valuable assistance was given in the preparation of this volume
by TIME-LIFE Correspondent Daniel Drooz, Jerusalem.

Published by TIME-LIFE International (Nederland) B.V.
5 Ottho Heldringstraat, Amsterdam 18.

*Cover*: Sunset in the Old City brings to sparkling life a gilded cross on one of Jerusalem's numerous churches.

*First end paper*: Persian tiles on the façade of the Muslim shrine known as the Dome of the Rock display Islamic script and floral patterns—even to the tip of a protruding water spout.

*Last end paper*: A section of an undulating house roof in the Old City of Jerusalem forms an abstract of stone blocks.

THE WORLD'S WILD PLACES
THE ART OF SEWING
THE OLD WEST
THE EMERGENCE OF MAN
LIFE LIBRARY OF PHOTOGRAPHY
TIME-LIFE LIBRARY OF ART
FOODS OF THE WORLD
GREAT AGES OF MAN
LIFE SCIENCE LIBRARY
LIFE NATURE LIBRARY

# Contents

# I

# The City of Earth and Heaven

Cities, like men, are shaped by the pressure of years and the violence of suffering. Some adapt and change, some are swept away—yet others preserve themselves despite every disaster, and of these none has clung to its character with such deep resilience as Jerusalem.

If the traveller stands, as I did not long ago, on the summit of the Mount of Olives, he sees all the ancient city stretched in front of him. It is, perhaps, the most awe-inspiring view in the world—for here lies the soul-city of an entire concept of God. Around Jerusalem the hills are bitterly eroded, their paths trodden bare by centuries of soldiers and peasantry. Once covered in forest, they are flecked now with little but rock and scentless scrub. To the south they fade into haze, dotted by weirdly beautiful villages, ripples of flat roofs lanced by minarets. To the east, far below, the Moab hills shine with a lunar emptiness over the Dead Sea, the deepest spot on earth. Between them and Jerusalem spreads the desert that the Hebrews called Yeshimon—"devastation". Its hills were a breeding-place of prophets, a refuge of exiles and bandits. They gave to the people a sense of living on the edge of doom.

In the clear Judean air the city appears closer than it is. It rests strangely quiet on its slopes. The circle of surrounding peaks lends a feeling of stillness, almost of sanctity, as if Jerusalem were indeed the centre of the world as medieval men believed. The immense and beautiful Turkish walls run along the hills like a part of the rock, and gather the houses of the Old City into a lake of roofs and domes.

As I gazed at the city, I could pick out landmarks that touched on three millennia of history. Outside the walls rose the unpretentious mound that King David captured 3,000 years ago, and that served the Israelites as capital for more than a millennium. Above it the city now was thick with the shrines of Christianity. And here, too, the lovely Islamic sanctuary called the Dome of the Rock proclaimed the triumph of the Muslim Arabs in A.D. 638.

Fount of three world religions—Judaism, Christianity, Islam—Jerusalem has entered the soul of half mankind. As Athens is to the mind, so is this city to the spirit. The idea that it nourished is now a commonplace, but was once a revelation—that God is a personal god, who cares about his people, loving their allegiance and hating their sins.

From the Mount of Olives I could see how hills had governed the form of the city. They swell to ridges from which the buildings stand up like symbols, then dip to half-invisible valleys. The walled city, old Jerusalem, is defended by such valleys on three sides. The suburbs are far larger, but lie

**Christian symbols of cross, thorns and chalice in the Dominus Flevit church overlook one of Islam's greatest shrines, the golden Dome of the Rock. The Dome itself stands on the site of the Temples of Solomon and Herod, sacred in the memory of the Jews.**

loose and scattered against it. To the north of the walls spreads a modest Arab quarter built without hurry among missions and church schools. To the west, Jewish Jerusalem, a city of more than two hundred thousand souls, has been pushed up at dizzy speed—a new Jerusalem that covers the slopes for over four miles.

Yet it is to the Old City that the eye returns (see map, pages 12/13). Clasped in its walls it is the city's heart, and it is beautiful with a hard compacted beauty: the place of Jesus, of Herod the Great, of Saladin. In the course of 3,000 years it has been conquered by Israelites and Baby-lonians, Greeks and Romans, Arabs, Seljuk Turks and Crusaders, the Mameluke slave-kings and the Ottoman Turks; and finally passed in this century out of the hands of the British and into those—once again—of the Jews. Like the irritant grain of sand in an oyster, the Old City has gathered its modern suburbs about it. But in the east and south, steep valleys with immemorial names—Kidron, Tyropoeon, Gehenna—still fall sharply away from its ramparts.

The one square-mile of the Old City lies across two hills: the eastern is Muslim—the western belongs to Christian Arabs, Armenians and Jews. The Muslim quarter is crowded about its principal shrine, the Dome of the Rock. In the west the Armenians—some two thousand—live in the seclusion of enormous convent walls, and a Jewish sector is growing beside them. To their north the Christian Arab quarter surrounds the Church of the Holy Sepulchre, built, it is held, where Christ was crucified and buried.

The present city was welded by the Six-Day War of 1967. After the British took Jerusalem from the Turks in 1917, their mandate brought deepening trouble between Arab and Jew, which exploded into conflict the moment they had departed. In 1949, after heavy fighting, the armistice line between the Arab kingdom of Jordan and the newly founded nation of Israel divided Jerusalem into two halves: the Arab Old City in the east, and the western city of the Jews. Not for 19 years—until Israel's victory in the Six-Day War—were the barriers cleared away. Then the two cities were united by roads, but not in spirit, and from where I stood on the Mount of Olives the signs of their trouble were even now below me in Jewish war memorials and desecrated graves.

In this there is nothing new. High above its valleys, Jerusalem is lifted on the carnage of its own centuries, layer upon layer of past destruction and daily waste. In the east, the walls built by the Turks rise on Roman stones that sometimes delve more than a hundred feet into the earth until they find solid rock. Age upon age, the city grows and is buried, and on the very site of the Temple of Solomon, now stands the Dome of the Rock.

Consecrated under the Dome is the rock-summit that is the city's core. Here the beliefs of Muslim and Jew converge. For this Rock, their traditions claim, is the foundation stone of the world. Upon it Adam was fashioned out of dust, Cain slew Abel, and Abraham prepared to sacrifice

A fatherly Abraham cradles in his ample lap members of Jerusalem's three faiths—Judaism, Christianity and Islam—in this 12th-Century illumination from a French Bible. Although the three religions differ radically, they all venerate the patriarch who broke from the worship of many gods to focus on one God alone.

Isaac. It was still a threshing-floor when David bought it with silver shekels for the site of the Temple that his son Solomon would build. For a thousand years the rock was the building's altar; long after the Temple's destruction the Arab conquerors proclaimed this to be the spot from which Muhammad journeyed by night to heaven.

Perhaps of all cities Jerusalem is the most intensely loved. Yet as in the days of Isaiah or of Jesus, it is bitter and divided, cruel even to its own, a caster out of prophets. When a person dies in the Arab quarter they sometimes say, "Jerusalem killed him".

To no other place does the traveller carry such expectations—and nowhere may they be more rudely shattered. The city is a revelation. Even its beauty has the clarity and strangeness of the surrounding rocks. It challenges a man on every side—his understanding, his spiritual faith, his political conscience. Here he may find his own religion revealed to him again, and he may be astonished or outraged by what he finds, even in its holiest places. For Jerusalem's lure is not gentleness nor even beauty, but the fascination of a past and a present that inspire and torture one another. This tension, the traveller feels, must have belonged to Jerusalem two and three thousand years ago. It lives in the very stones.

To begin to comprehend such a city, a man must turn back almost 40 centuries to a time when the Nile and the Euphrates watered half civilization. Then, along the divide between myth and history, a small tribe of herdsmen, travelling southwards over the Syrian desert, arrived at a hill-town whose inhabitants welcomed their leader with gifts of corn and wine. This moment of hospitality marks the earliest contact of Jerusalem with the two peoples who were to love and fight over it. For the nomad leader, Abraham, was in legend the ancestor of both Jew and Arab. In his person they were once united and at peace.

Looked at from the vantage point of today this earliest gift of the city seems to belong to a time of primal innocence. The Jews, who turned Jerusalem into a symbol of fulfilment, spoke of a city transfigured at the end of time and governed by a king of light who would reconcile all nations. They came to conceive a "Jerusalem of the Upper World". Ever since then the worldly city and "the Jerusalem of the heart"—the actual and the ideal —have existed side by side.

The earthly Jerusalem, of course, was more vulnerable. In exile the Jews believed it to be very different from the reality. To them its very stones were perfect, its people wise, its women beautiful. On Judgement Day it would blossom into gardens and be ringed with walls of gold and lazulite, emerald and fire. God and His angels would circle it with their wings, and the nations of the earth be carried there on clouds.

This yearning, the desire of man to transcend his mortality, was inherited by Christianity. St. John, St. Paul, St. Augustine all wrote of a mystical city

**A trick of light on a misty winter day trims sprawling Jerusalem to the proportions of the old walled city. On the hills beyond rise the tall blocks of the modern Jewish suburbs, while in the foreground stand houses built upon the site of earliest Jerusalem, the city David conquered and made the capital of the Israelites.**

that would one day pour its ideal upon earth. "It is evident from the testimony of even heathen witnesses", wrote an early church father about Jerusalem, "that in Judea there was a city suspended in the sky early every morning for forty days. As the day advanced, the entire figure of the walls would wane gradually, and sometimes it would vanish instantly."

When the Muslims became masters of the city in the 7th Century they too came to believe it greater than itself. From its holy Rock, they said, Muhammad rose into the sky and was shown all the spheres of paradise; and the seventh heaven of Islam was conceived as a counterpart of Jerusalem's holy mountain.

After the waning of medieval Christianity, the vision dimmed but did not die. It found its way into the background of Renaissance canvases, in which painters reflected their own countries. The Florentines cluttered it with Tuscan trees and campaniles. Dürer drew a Rhenish Jerusalem complete with windmills and Gothic turrets; Mantegna's city stood under brooding mountains. Writers and theologians conceived still another vision exemplified by the English poet Blake:

I saw the New Jerusalem descending out of Heaven
Between thy Wings of gold and silver, feather'd immortal,
Clear as the rainbow . . .

But what, meanwhile, of Jerusalem on earth?

Since the time of Christ a dozen civilizations had built it up or thrown it down, sowing new streets and shrines until the city that one century knew became blurred in the upsurge of the next. As the Eastern Roman Empire dwindled, Arab invaders from the south seized the city in A.D. 638. Thereafter, except for the brief Crusader conquest, Jerusalem belonged to the Muslims (to Arab dynasties at first, then to the Mameluke slave-kings of Egypt). And after the Turkish victories of 1517, an indolent Ottoman administration took its toll for 400 years. Christian pilgrims returned with tales of hardship and corruption. And even now to the innocent traveller's ideal the city may give a disturbing reply: the harshness of man and God. Is this, he may wonder, his city? Is this even his God?

I descended the Mount of Olives, passing beneath the walls of Christian sanctuaries thronged with bougainvillea and pines. They marked sad sites. Here Jesus wept over the city. Here he knelt in prayer. Here he was betrayed. In half an hour I reached the Damascus Gate, the threshold of Old Jerusalem, and plunged into its ferment. The only transport to navigate these choked alleys is that of donkeys and hand-wheeled carts. The rest is a river of people. Some are slim and hawkish as the classic Bedouin, others squat and heavy-nosed; still others have blue eyes or red hair—in the case of Arabs, a Circassian or Crusader heritage—or the wide Mongol face of the Anatolian Turk.

I saw a Negro shoe-seller, descendant from Bedouin or Ottoman slaves, lying under a wall and crying his wares with a shrill "Ee-hoo!" Up the Via

An Arab watch-seller—one of many pedlars who take up stations along Jerusalem's narrow streets—rests in the afternoon shade while keeping a predatory eye out for passing tourists. Although dressed Western style, he has on an Arab cap and wears his checkered kaffiyeh or head-dress like a scarf round his neck.

Dolorosa, the traditional route of Christ to Calvary, flowed a crowd of Palestinian countrywomen, graceful in their embroidered dresses and white head veils. I turned to stare at an Armenian priest and collided with a Franciscan monk. Hasidic Jews, pale men who seemed to see nothing around them, were making their way to the Wailing Wall. Behind them came United Nations soldiers from Peru, an Arab porter hunched double under his load, Israeli policemen, a stray sheep, an Abyssinian monk, and a group of urbane Orthodox priests. And all this river of humanity, swelled by a flood of tourists, is propelled along ways sometimes so narrow that three men cannot walk abreast.

The shops are open to the street in the oriental way. Most of them are little more than booths, and their wares hang on every wall so that at one moment I wandered through a jungle of carpets and sheepskin coats, the next brushed against butchers' carcasses or ducked among Palestinian dresses, cascades of pseudo-Bedouin jewellery and rosaries.

In a lonelier street I found myself walking beside a gentle-faced librarian, a Jew, and fell into conversation with him. One thing, I told him, I had noticed: Arab and Jew did not walk together. "But we Israelis get on well with Arabs," he answered. "Haven't you seen us working side by side? On building sites, in cafés, everywhere. It's only politics that have divided us. Slogans, governments, artificial things."

"So the Arabs are happy with this?"

"Well," he looked down cautiously at the book he was carrying, "their happiness will come. We give them employment and social benefits. Once they forget Arab propaganda, we will live well together. We will have peace."

"How long", I asked, "before then?"

"The Arabs have no education, that's the trouble—no industry, no commerce. When we came to this country, what was it good for?" He tapped his book. "But the Jewish people, you see, had a will. That is the difference. We made something of this land. Today the merest Arab labourer can earn handsomely on our building sites. They even send children to work on the sites—children who should be in school. Our police have to send them away. What sort of people is that, who will not educate their children?"

"Yet you will live together?"

He turned in the entrance to a newly-rebuilt synagogue. "In time. Yes, in time." He gave a fragile smile. "Things will be forgotten."

The confusion and paradox of the city are like no other. At times above the Wailing Wall you may hear church bells, Muslim prayer-calls and Jewish chanting. Every quarter clings to its personality. On Fridays the Muslim sector is shuttered and deserted, on Saturdays the Jewish, on Sundays the Christian. The religious sects and sub-sects are almost too many to be numbered. Festivals follow one another feverishly.

I peered into one of the shops. Its Arab keeper tried to sell me a dagger, then a crucifix, then a Jewish candlestick. "You sell Israeli things?" I asked.

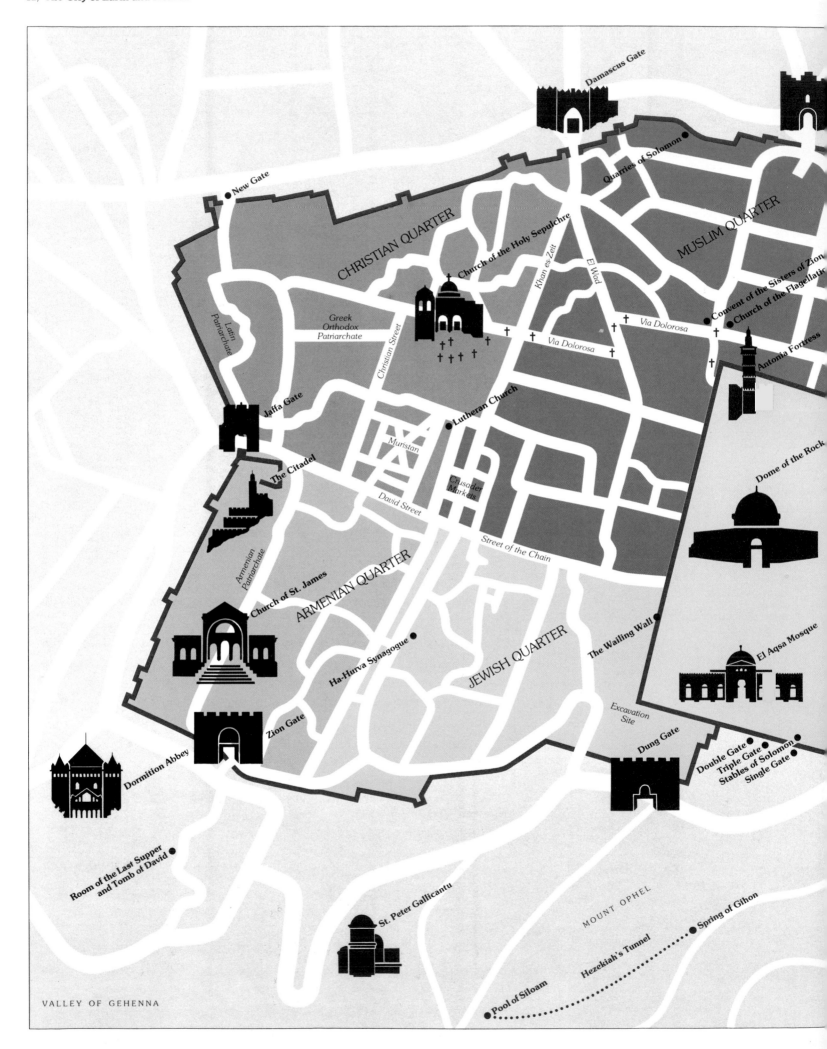

Damascus Gate

Quarries of Solomon

CHRISTIAN QUARTER

MUSLIM QUARTER

New Gate

Church of the Holy Sepulchre

Khan es-Zeit

El Wad

Convent of the Sisters of Zion

Church of the Flagellation

Greek
Orthodox
Patriarchate

Latin Patriarchate

Via Dolorosa

Via Dolorosa

Christian Street

Antonia Fortress

Jaffa Gate

Lutheran Church

Muristan

The Citadel

Crusader
Markets

Dome of the Rock

David Street

Armenian
Patriarchate

Street of the Chain

Church of St. James

ARMENIAN QUARTER

El Aqsa Mosque

Ha-Hurva Synagogue

JEWISH QUARTER

The Wailing Wall

Zion Gate

Excavation
Site

Dung Gate

Double Gate
Triple Gate
Stables of Solomon
Single Gate

Dormition Abbey

Room of the Last Supper
and Tomb of David

St. Peter Gallicantu

MOUNT OPHEL

Spring of Gihon

Hezekiah's Tunnel

VALLEY OF GEHENNA

Pool of Siloam

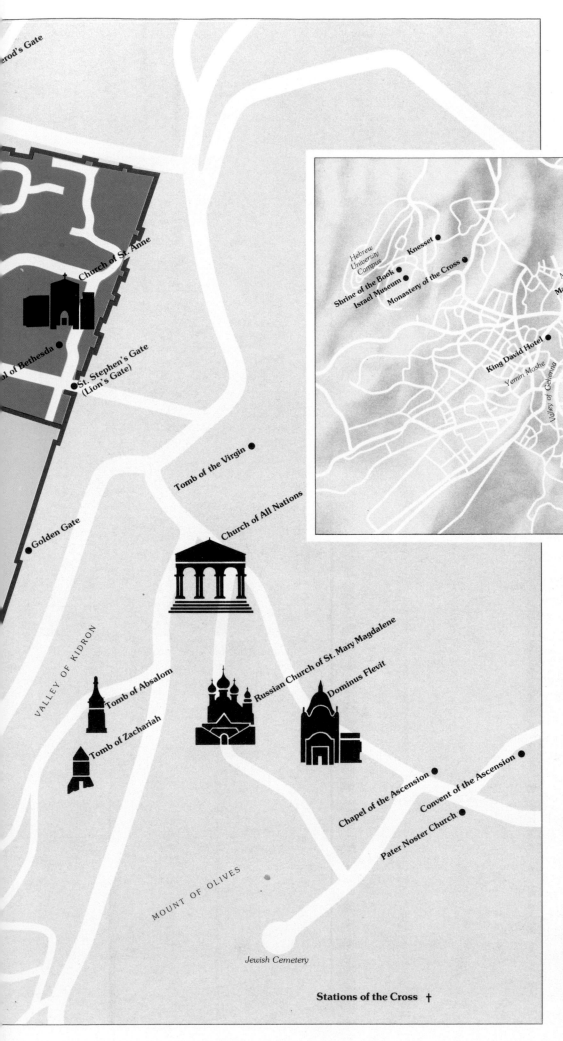

Herod's Gate

Church of St. Anne

ol of Bethesda

St. Stephen's Gate
(Lion's Gate)

Tomb of the Virgin

Golden Gate

Church of All Nations

VALLEY OF KIDRON

Tomb of Absalom

Russian Church of St. Mary Magdalene

Dominus Flevit

Tomb of Zachariah

Convent of the Ascension

Chapel of the Ascension

Pater Noster Church

MOUNT OF OLIVES

Jewish Cemetery

**Stations of the Cross** †

Mount Scopus

Hebrew University Campus

Knesset

Shrine of the Book
Israel Museum

Monastery of the Cross

Mea Shearim

Mandelbaum Gate

St. Stephen's Church

Rockefeller Museum

Christian Quarter

Muslim Quarter

King David Hotel

Yemin Moshe

Armenian Quarter

Jewish Quarter

Garden of Gethsemane

Valley of Gehenna

Mount Ophel

Valley of Kidron

Mount of Olives

Hill of Evil Counsel

Village of Silwan
Mount of Offence

## The City of Religions

Jerusalem consists of two parts—the Old City within its 400-year-old Turkish walls, the subject of the larger simplified map at left, and the newer city to the north and west of the walls (see inset above). The Old City itself is divided into four religious quarters—Christian, Armenian, Jewish and Muslim—whose boundaries have been rendered only approximately here.

Shown on the map of the Old City and the inset are shrines, monuments, institutions, thoroughfares (in outsized scale) and topographical features described or mentioned in this book. Most important among these are the Church of the Holy Sepulchre in the Old City, around which lies the Christian quarter; the Wailing Wall or Western Wall at the edge of the Jewish quarter; and the adjacent area of the Dome of the Rock, nearly half as big as the Muslim quarter that nestles against it. Wandering through the Muslim quarter and into the Christian quarter is the Via Dolorosa, the route that, by tradition, Christ followed on his way to Calvary; crosses along it and inside the confines of the Church of the Holy Sepulchre mark the 14 Stations of the Cross.

He avoided my stare. "A man has to eat. I have a family. Five children." He spread out his hands helplessly. "What can we do? We are slave-people now." But he looked too tired to be angry.

Only business, I thought, might ease the two peoples together. I fingered his poorly woven carpets.

"Everything's more expensive now." His voice turned harsh. "A camel stays a camel, a man stays a man but a pound doesn't stay a pound." A pair of orthodox Jews stopped outside the shop, then moved on. "Our people take work from the Israelis because they have to. They've no choice."

"You can't grow to like them?"

He jerked back his head in denial. "We pass one another in the street, Arab and Jew, that's all. If they question us, we answer. No more." He fingered the Jewish candlestick. "None of us here minds whether we belong to Jordan, Egypt or Palestine—what does it matter? So long as we're ruled by Arabs." With a dark bitterness, he added: "Only take away Israel. That's all we ask. Set us free from Israel."

Back in the bazaars the press of peoples thrown together was suffocating. The August heat fell pitiless out of a pure sky. The smells of charcoal, leather, pastries, hides, spices, excrement stifled the air. From every other shop a farrago of religious souvenirs glared in silver, olive wood and mother-of-pearl: Crusader crosses, Maltese crosses, stars of David, seven-branched candelabra, Christian fishes, hands to ward off the Evil Eye, even pendants inscribed "God bless this House" for Anglican pilgrims.

Out of these lanes ran thinner ones, splashed with lonely sunlight. In worn steps they climbed up and down the city's smothered slopes. And here I could see that all the crude modernity of merchandise hung upon Arab arches, Crusader vaults, Turkish walls, stubs of Roman columns—their surfaces worn smooth and shining.

Amid such history the people live and work and worship. Outside the city walls, where the houses, however small, are built pleasantly in lime-stone and show gardens of flowering shrubs and pine, a feeling of light and air pervades Jerusalem. But inside the Old City the Arab houses overlap and lean upon one another in a chaos of centuries, and their courtyards are crushed and small, flagged in stone without a flower or tree.

Their doors give directly on to the streets and sometimes, as I walked, finding one ajar, I would creak it open and peer into dank passageways or up flights of steps. Muffled voices sounded in thick-walled chambers. Starved cats flew among shadows. If the stranger is asked inside he finds the rooms almost heartrendingly empty. Unless a family has inherited some solid peasant furniture or the elaborate tables and carpets of Otto-man times, it lives among a few sticks of modernity—for the taste of the poor is invariably for something new. The walls show garish pictures, or nothing. A handful of treasures stands proudly in a cabinet—chinaware, ornaments, gifts from relatives emigrated abroad. In the kitchen you may

An Arab schoolboy glances back into the shadows of an arched passageway. Such crooked, narrow streets, many with stone steps, lace the Old City. The ramp facilitates handcarts delivering goods to houses and shops.

stumble with amazement upon a huge, gleaming washing-machine or refrigerator, for which all other comforts have for years been sacrificed.

The Arabs live, on average, more than two to a room, and many houses have no indoor lavatory, let alone a bath. Seventeen per cent of their babies still die in infancy, and although children must now attend school at the age of five, I have often wandered through streets filled with tatterdemalions fighting and shouting, pestering and scavenging. As I walked, I observed these children. Above spidery legs and ragged bodies their faces were already old. Only the eyes, liquid and very dark, showed in repose a half-melancholy innocence. In these congested alleys, whose homes are too small for much activity, both work and leisure are public.

Tourism is the Old City's heavy industry. Its people, typically, are textile workers, souvenir-vendors, restaurateurs. And their prey is the foreigner. He wanders among them, besieged. In a hundred shops he is confronted by the same glitter; pseudo-Jewish, hybrid Muslim, commercial Christian; copper from Acre, brass from Nazareth, grandiose Iranian silverware, boxes encrusted in a sickly mother-of-pearl from Bethlehem. "Olive wood from Gethsemane" is rife. It encloses Bibles and prayer books or erupts into figures of the Holy Family, the Venus de Medici and a host of synthetic biblical sages. The harsh graining of the wood lends all the carvings the same doleful expressions. Other shops sell nothing but candles: gilded and coagulated candles, flat candles, candles like coral or towers: all hideous.

Then there are the dealers in antiquities. They sit behind their wares, showily perusing museum catalogues, until they have gauged the ignorance of their clients, and sleekly suggest a Roman lamp or a Syrian vase. True antiquities are expensive, and now that Muslim pilgrims can no longer pass through Jerusalem, the more modest goods they used to sell— old pots and rugs—have vanished. The best things are the simplest: basketwork, copper kitchen ware, pottery, the plainer Hebron glass.

If the average worker of the new city outside is a Jewish clerk or administrator, the archetype of the Old City is the Arab shopkeeper or craftsman, a person at once child-like and sophisticated, impulsive and circumspect. He is generally his own master, living by the skin of his teeth and the quick of his brain. You may see him selling anything from fake icons to clay jars, making jewellery or tooling leather, wandering the lanes with circles of sesame-sprinkled bread balanced in a tray upon his head, or standing at his iron foundry—there are more than 70 in the Arab city—hammering sparks from old girders or bedsteads to turn junk to new uses.

Towards evening, as I walked along the Old City's arteries—the streets of El-Wad and Khan es-Zeit, Christian and David Street—its people were taking their traditional leisure, seated in the coffee shops on reed-bottomed chairs, with their small cups placed delicately on other chairs in front of them, or cradled in their hands. Some played backgammon with histrionic cries and gestures, so that small crowds gathered about them.

The realm of biblical seers and prophets, the eroded Judean Hills to the east of Jerusalem stretch to the horizon in parched desolation. This is the so-called wilderness where John the Baptist preached and Jesus came to fast and to meditate for 40 days and 40 nights.

Others talked in the murmurous privacy with which Levantine peoples discuss politics, grouped in sad and vaguely suspicious circles. Tired and older men, their heads swathed in the Arab *kaffiyeh* or crowned with a fez, sucked on their hookahs in silence and fell asleep.

People have rarely lived to a great age here. Even before his sixties an Arab may gather in his face all the sags and lines of a century. When I leaned for a moment in a doorway and watched passers-by, I noticed how many lame there were. Jerusalem's medical services are today among the best in the Middle East, yet the past still weighs heavy here: every second person looked sick in body, and up and down the hill-alleys the sticks of the blind tapped incessantly.

I made my way into the Christian quarter near the Church of the Holy Sepulchre. The streets were filled with monks and Jewish tourists, and Arab masons covered in dust were driving their loaded donkeys up the lanes. The presence of so many priests gave the feeling of a religious convocation. Their sandals crunched and slapped in the dust. Their robes and cowls brushed between Israeli soldiers and Americans in jeans. The Christian Arab shopkeepers—a little wealthier than their Muslim counterparts, a little more suave—murmured greetings and invitations. In such streets, where all traffic goes on foot, the human voice—arguing, muttering, cajoling—is the loudest sound heard.

From the Church of the Holy Sepulchre, the most sacred sanctuary in Christendom, it is a five-minute walk to the Wailing Wall, the holiest site of Jewry; and above the Wall, the Dome of the Rock—one of Islam's greatest shrines—flowers to the sky. From these three monuments, like planted seeds, the Christian, Jewish and Muslim quarters have grown. And if the Christian is commercial and the Muslim crowded and poor, the Jewish quarter is fiercely rebuilding itself as a symbol of national redemption.

Immediately after the Six-Day War the Moroccan quarter around the Wailing Wall was blown up to clear a space for worship. Now the sun beats shadowless on a vast and blinding pavement. The Wall rises hugely beyond it, and high above the golden Dome of the Rock shines like a setting sun.

The size and permanence of the Wall are Roman, built in the calm of a great empire. But if you stand closer, you see that for all their mass these stones are sympathetic, individual. Some, cut from the hard *mezze* limestone, have kept their edges sharp and perfect. Others, scooped from the softer *malaky*, are wrinkled like hands along the veins of their weakness, horizontal or vertical as they were laid, or have split savagely inward through their entire depth. Against their eternity the men murmur and sway in prayer. Their heads reach only to the second course of stones. Their hands touch them with an automatic love. Sometimes a wind comes to twirl their prayer-shawls about their shoulders or ruffle the pages of their books. But their worship stays private and intense. Each seems to hold communion with the ancient stone in front of him.

One legend tells that when Solomon erected the Temple he assigned the building of each part to a different class and that this Wall was raised by the beggars. On the day of the Temple's destruction angels linked their wings about the Wall and cried: "This, the work of the poor, shall never be destroyed." Since then the Divine Presence has never left it, and on dewy evenings they say the stones weep for the Temple's fall.

On some days, especially during the confirmation of boys, the Wall becomes a theatre of rejoicing. The tapping of hand-drums and the ululation of the women, craning over the barrier that separates them from the men, drowns out the sad bray of the *shofar* horn. Piety and tourism mingle. While the Orthodox sway and murmur as if drunk with their prayer, Jews from America or France photograph one another in borrowed skull caps.

But usually the place is almost silent. At noon the slanting sun, swinging vertical to the stones, picks out every crease in them, while pigeons waddle in their crevices. Only on festivals, and on the anniversary of the Temple's fall, does the whisper of the faithful swell to a confused, heart-rending roar.

"For the palace that lies desolate," cries one.

*"We sit in solitude and mourn,"* the chorus answers.

"For the walls that are overthrown,
*We sit in solitude and mourn.*
For our glory which is departed,
For our wise men who have perished,
For the priests who have stumbled,
For our kings who have despised Him. . . .
*We sit in solitude and mourn."*

In Jerusalem, more evidently than anywhere, man is bound to his past—a past which is all about him, in every stone and trampled hill. Yet the very richness of this past is daunting to the stranger. How to understand such a tumult of peoples, buildings, beliefs? In a single street may walk men of 20 different sects, in whose faces you may see the blood of Turkish soldiers, Byzantine merchants, Crusader knights. Well may the traveller ask in bewilderment if he will ever understand such a place.

Only history can explain—a history still alive in flesh and rock. And it is this that I will set out to explore—not by cold research, but by walking streets and meeting men.

# The Vibrant Life of Old Jerusalem

**Joined by the patron (centre) outside his café, men wearing kaffiyehs sit in the sunshine and shade and indulge an Arab passion: animated conversation.**

The Old City within its Turkish walls is the heart of sprawling Jerusalem. In the crowded compass of one square mile, more than 25,000 inhabitants are gathered into its four religious quarters—a confusion of stone buildings, mingled and superimposed over the centuries and threaded by intricate alleys. Shops, stalls and workshops line narrow streets, some of which still follow straight courses laid down in Roman times, and a constant traffic of handcarts and donkeys competes with crowds of sellers and buyers, workers and sightseers. The Arab quarter shown in these photographs harbours the Old City's commercial life. Even in the cosmopolitan turmoil of tourists, pilgrims and Israelis, it is the Arab population—clinging to older ways—that contributes most of the colour and the tempo to the daily life of the 4,000-year-old city.

**Beneath stone arches dating from medieval times, a milling crowd of shoppers and tourists fills David Street, one of the Old City's main thoroughfares.**

Against a background of posters, a vendor sells bread, eggs and felafel—an Arab labourer's breakfast.

Shoeshines are offered at a polished brass stand.

A juice seller dispenses his refreshments by pipette.

## A Vivid Commerce

Business life in the Old City takes place mainly outdoors. Shops, often no more than booths or recesses in walls, are open from early morning until sunset. Street vendors change their station with the rhythm of demand as the tides of workers and tourists ebb and flow. Most of the traders are men; following tradition, Muslim women try to keep out of sight within the warren of shadowy buildings and courtyards.

Two Muslim women stroll along El-Wad, another of the Old City's thoroughfares. They are veiled in strict adherence to Muslim orthodoxy. But the little girls skipping past in school smocks belong to the world of today, and will grow up to wear Western clothes.

A bakery boy delivers a tray of bread to a café.

A sheet of plywood arrives at a carpenter's workshop.

A large-screen television set makes a heavy load.

Empty crates nearly overwhelm this bowed porter.

## Deliveries by Manpower

Through narrow, stepped lanes where motor traffic is an impossibility, much of the transport is by the simplest method: a man carrying a burden. Among the traders and roundsmen, professional porters are identifiable by their protective head cloths and leather or sackcloth jerkins. Hired either by the day or by the job, they tread steadily up and down the intricate alleys, often bent double under loads that would fill a small van.

Bending beneath his sombre load, a porter carries a coffin of rough boards, its lid ominously agape. Its destination: a Christian dwelling, where a man has died.

**Shielded from the late sun by a café's half-lowered shutter, two young Arabs study their newspapers.**

**Two intense café customers pursue a conversation, seemingly unaware of their spartan surroundings.**

# Café Society

Arab cafés are an integral part of the life of the streets. Tourists bypass their stark undecorated interiors, but every café has its regular customers among the men who turn in for a talk and a smoke at all hours of the day. Small cups of coffee or mint tea may punctuate their conversation, but they can talk on for hours over an empty table, or sit with a cigarette or bubbling water-pipe, silent and undisturbed.

In a quiet corner an elderly Arab reflectively smokes his narghile, or water-pipe. Local tobacco is employed, sometimes combined with a little hashish.

A solitary orthodox Jew, picked out by the light of dawn, walks through a still-shuttered Muslim street on his way to pray at the Wailing Wall.

# 2

# The Place of David

Jerusalem existed even before the time of Abraham, but today's city has slowly moved to northward of the earliest settlement. The original city is now little more than an eroded hillock that successive archaeologists have laid bare. To tramp its rough terraces is to be astonished that this place should have contained in its small compass the religious destiny of half the world. For it was the modest hill of Ophel that David made capital of a united Israel. But of the city he knew, only ambiguous ruins remain above ground, and if I were to rediscover its past I would have to probe for evidence more deeply buried, cut in the rock of the hill itself: tunnels, water-shafts, quarries, cave-tombs.

Such a past goes back immeasurably far, to a time when men conceived elemental deities: star gods and sky fathers, mothers of the earth and corn. Not until about 1000 B.C. did a group of Semitic tribes, the Israelites, come to believe in a different sort of God: a Moral Being who guided His people's steps and saw into their hearts. This God—loving, just and incorruptible— was to be inherited, in different guises, by the two great religions that followed: Christianity and Islam.

Touched by the older wisdom of Babylon and Egypt yet holding to the concept of their own deity, the Israelites wandered in the Sinai desert, emerging at last on the rim of Canaan, a fertile country split among petty kings. For 200 years they infiltrated its farmlands and fought against its cities, whose chariot-driving lords proved a formidable adversary.

Eventually the Israelites did gain the ascendancy; but then a new enemy appeared. These were men of uncertain origin, iron-bearing strangers called Philistines who marched southwards down the Mediterranean coast with ox-carts and a fleet of high-prowed ships sailing alongside. In the face of their threat the Israelites, whose 12 tribes were constantly feuding with one another, were forced to unite or be destroyed. And it was now, as they banded together in self-defence, that they found their land weakened at the centre by an enclave of hostile Jebusites—an obscure people whose capital was the hill-town of Jerusalem. The Israelites, under their warrior-king David, laid siege to the city and took it for their own.

The ruins of this earliest settlement lie outside the present ramparts where the Kidron and Tyropoeon Valleys meet at the hill of Ophel. The stone terraces are drifting to rubble, but at their feet the clear spring of Gihon still flows. Close by, its boulders piled on virgin rock, is the base of the Jebusite wall-tower that guarded the spring. Clambering over these stones, laid over three millennia ago, I understood the insolence of the

**Absorbed in his prayer book, an old Jew sits close by the Moroccan Gate leading to the site of the ancient Jewish Temples. His orthodoxy demands that he does not visit the area, where now the Dome of the Rock stands, for fear of treading on the sacred ground that was the Temples' Holy of Holies.**

Jebusites—for when David besieged them they taunted him by shouting down that their lame and blind would be sufficient to defend the walls.

David expressed in his person all that his followers admired. A man of military prowess and practical intelligence, who spread his conquests from Sinai to the Euphrates, he was devoted to his people's God, and as a poet and a harpist he could touch their souls. The Bible indicates that he did not storm Jerusalem, but took it by stealth. The Jebusites had channelled the waters of the Gihon spring deep into the hill of Ophel, and could reach them with buckets dropped through a shaft from the city above. Into this spring, and up the vertical shaft, David sent a force of commandos. "And David said on that day, whosoever getteth up the gutter, and smiteth the Jebusites, and the lame and the blind that are hated of David's soul, he shall be chief and captain." And his own nephew Joab, adds the Book of Chronicles, "went first up and was chief".

Today, if you climb down into the Gihon spring, the water reaching to your waist, and wade along the Jebusite tunnel for 70 feet into the hill, you will see at its end, high above you in your torchlight, the way by which David's men ascended 3,000 years before.

Because Jerusalem lay in no one's tribal territory, David selected it to unite the 12 Israelite tribes into one nation. Like the Vatican or Olympia it was designed to transcend petty jealousies, and to symbolize instead a religious ideal. So the holy Ark, which contained on inscribed tablets the Ten Commandments given to Moses on Sinai, was carried into the city. And David himself danced before it in ritual, to harps and cymbals.

When David died, he left behind him on the hill of Ophel a town little changed. As I tramped over its meagre 11 acres of dust and pines I could see nothing that he had built. Its slopes, centuries later, had been quarried by the Romans into ferocious geometric shapes. I stumbled across a surrealist landscape of hewn pits filled with litter. From the valley opposite, where the village of Silwan climbed among rock-tombs, the sound of women's voices echoed with a magical distinctness. Soon I was walking among remains of sepulchres half cut away. Deep entranceways showed in the rock. Staircases led to nothing. It is not known who was entombed here: but in the earliest years of the kingdom, none but monarchs could be interred within the city, and as each ruler died, the Bible records that he "slept with his fathers and was buried in the city of David".

Now the shafts were filled with goats' dung and their ceilings blackened by the fires of generations of nomads. As I peered into one shaft, I surprised a tiny Arab girl. She was playing with a plastic doll. She gave me a frightened glance and breathed, "Help!" Then she collected herself, cradled her doll in her arms—as if it, and not she, had been scared—and skittered away whispering to it, "Don't worry."

I examined the tomb she had left. It contained a cavity for a sarcophagus, wide but very short: its king could have been scarcely five feet tall. I dug a

Ancient olive trees grow in tiers on crumbling terraces that criss-cross the slopes under the Old City's eastern walls. For centuries olives have been the main agricultural yield of the rocky hill country around Jerusalem.

heel into the depression, but there was nothing now except dust, in the place where David himself might have been laid.

It was David's son, Solomon, who plucked the fruit of his father's conquests. In these two men—the one a pragmatic soldier-king, the other a royal voluptuary veiled in wisdom and splendour—the brief glory of Israel touches its zenith and hints at its end.

Within David's reign alone the Israelites acquired an empire, a navy and a huge trade—all the stuff of power and trouble. To match this worldly grandeur, Solomon built the Temple whose opulence and beauty so amazed his people. David had chosen its site before his death: a threshing-floor that overlooked the city, and that the Israelites came to know as Mount Moriah, "the Vision of God". Here Solomon raised a shrine of jointed lime-stone, cedarwood and gold. The awe of the semi-nomadic Israelites can still be sensed in the Bible, as they watched the Temple's parts created one by one at the hands of foreign craftsmen: walls, ceilings and folding doors gilded with palms and flowers, great brass oxen whose backs upheld the ablutions pool outside, and enormous cherubim that touched their wings above the Ark in the dark of the inner sanctuary—the Holy of Holies. For the Israelites knew nothing of such things, and these wonders were created by draughtsmen whom Solomon had hired from the Phoenicians of Lebanon, a sea-going people old in artistry. Yet inside the Holy of Holies, inscribed upon the tablets and enclosed by the Ark, was an ethical code more profound than anything the Phoenicians knew. It spoke of duty and order, mercy and honour.

Solomon's Temple, his cedarwood palace adorned by golden shields, his harem and his throne-room were destroyed long ago. But the Temple may have left behind it a curious relic that was not rediscovered until the last century. In 1852 an Englishman, James Barclay, was walking his dog along the northern walls of Jerusalem when the dog vanished. After a while Barclay saw it re-emerge as if out of the rock of the scarp. He went to investigate, and noticed an entrance hidden by shrubs and stones. To his amazement he found himself wandering in a vast subterranean quarry whose walls gleamed snow-white and still showed the marks of chisels and even of niches where workmen had hung their lamps. Who had excavated this labyrinth? Nobody could be sure; but these were probably the quarries worked by Herod the Great and perhaps by King Solomon before him.

As I descended into their caverns, I saw others opening before me—a whole network of vast, interconnecting chambers. They were dimly lit by electric lamps strung together along the ground. At first the caves spread low, upheld on pillars of natural rock; then they broke into galleries where smaller caves multiplied into the gloom, or came to a sudden end at walls littered with chippings. By now I was walking deep beneath the crowded streets of the Old City; but I could hear only the drip of water from faintly glistening ceilings, and the sound of a distant spring.

## The First 4,000 Years

Few cities have survived so many disasters as Jerusalem. Conquered by one people after another, razed and rebuilt time and time again, the city has undergone a never-ending process of renewal. Important dates in its history are noted here in a chronology that touches upon highlights recounted or mentioned in this book.

| | |
|---|---|
| B.C. 19th Century | First recorded mention of Jerusalem |
| c. 996 | David takes Jerusalem and makes it the capital of the Israelites |
| 961 | Reign of King Solomon, and building of the first Temple |
| 587 | Nebuchadnezzar destroys Jerusalem; the Exile in Babylon begins for the Jews |
| 539 | Cyrus of Persia permits the Jews to return from their captivity |
| 332 | Alexander the Great conquers the Persian Empire, Ptolemaic Dynasty of Egypt rules Jerusalem |
| 198 | Control of Jerusalem passes to the Graeco-Syrian Seleucids |
| 168 | Antiochus Epiphanes desecrates the Temple |
| 167 | Jewish revolt, led by the Maccabees, begins |
| 63 | Pompey captures Jerusalem for Rome |
| 37-4 | The reign of King Herod the Great; rebuilding of the Temple |
| A.D. 26-36 | Procuratorship of Pontius Pilate |
| c. 30 | Crucifixion of Jesus |
| 70 | Titus razes Jerusalem and the Temple |
| 132-5 | Second revolt of the Jews |

The extent of this maze was formidable. Out of its rough and pallid limestone must have come half a city: temples, fortresses, palaces. I felt lost in their void. For just as a whole town could be built from such a quarry, so a whole underground world is created in the process. Sometimes the walls stood out in sharp, vertical clusters, like the columns of a cathedral; sometimes the space dwindled to grottoes that looked nearly natural, as if scooped out all of a piece. I was walking through one of these chambers when I realized that I was not alone.

Somebody was moving over loose stones in the darkness of a pit below. Soon I saw a light flash and heard mumbling. In a moment, a fat figure in shirt-sleeves appeared and stared up at me, perplexed. "I can't find the tunnel," he called up. "Have you seen the tunnel?" He clambered towards me. "The tunnel of King Zedekiah. Where he escaped."

The man turned out to be an elderly Polish Jew; in spite of the quarry's coldness he was sweating. "There's no tunnel," I said. "It's a legend."

"But it is written!" he insisted. "King Zedekiah escaped from the Babylonians here. He followed a tunnel which came out at Jericho."

"But Jericho's 20 miles away."

He answered: "All the same, it is written."

As far as I could remember it was written only in legend. The Bible says that the Israelite king fled through the city gates and that at Jericho he was captured by the Babylonians, who slew his sons in front of his eyes—before blinding him, and taking his people into captivity.

But the old man was determined to find the tunnel. He explained that he had lived in Poland for most of his life, and he had seen nothing like these works of his ancestors. Surely they were capable of anything? "When I see what my people did, I am proud, so proud." He seemed close to tears. "At the Wailing Wall," he went on, "there is a place where you can look down and see how far the Temple went into the ground. How did they do such things? How?"

He picked up one of the lights which hung loose on its cord along the path, and trained it over the rock. But only the strange, white pillars answered him. I noticed with a start that there was a concentration camp number pricked on the inside of his forearm. "The passage must be somewhere. What was 20 miles to such people?" He wandered away from me, scrutinizing the dark and muttering to himself, "Besides, it is written".

I emerged into the dazzling light. If the quarries are truly those of Solomon, they are all that is left of his Temple: a giant absence. The place where the altar stood is protected now by the Dome of the Rock, and shows nothing but an expanse of stone, indecipherably scarred. When I returned to the hill of Ophel, I saw that not more than a foot separated the Jebusite rampart that David stormed from the wall that succeeded it in the 8th Century B.C. In this tiny glade of space and time, where now a few butterflies fidgeted among thistles, the power of Israel declined. During these hard centuries the kingdom divided. The ten northern tribes split from the two southern ones, and looked to Samaria, 40 miles to the north, as their capital. Jerusalem remained head of only a tiny kingdom. The Temple was pillaged by the Egyptians, even by the northern tribes. But at the same time, in the face of foreign threat and their people's infidelity, a succession of prophets spoke of a loving and a universal God beside whom all other gods were baubles of the imagination.

In 722 B.C. the northern tribes of Israel vanished under the weight of Assyria, and were never heard of again. Twenty years later, when the army of the terrible Assyrian monarch Sennacherib descended on Jerusalem, the Judean King Hezekiah looked to the city's defences. Above all, he decided to deprive the Assyrians of water. "And when Hezekiah saw that Senna-cherib was come," runs the Book of Chronicles, "and he was purposed to fight against Jerusalem, he took counsel with his princes and his mighty men to stop the water of the fountains which were without the city . . . saying, 'Why should the kings of Assyria come, and find much water?'"

Not only did Hezekiah conceal the wells outside Jerusalem, but he set two gangs of workmen tunnelling towards each other from either side of the hill of Ophel. Through the passage that they cut, deep under the hill, the waters of the Gihon fountain were led into the city.

This fountain, where Solomon had been anointed king 250 years before, still flows into a cave-pool at the foot of Ophel, bubbling beneath a flight of worn steps. Its current is strangely intermittent and for as long as ten hours at a time it almost stops. The Arabs, who call it "the Spring of the Mother of Steps", say that beneath the pool lives a dragon that swallows the waters, and that when the dragon falls asleep they run again.

Cavernous limestone quarries that run 250 yards into the heart of the hill beneath the Old City were cut in the 1st Century B.C. by Herod's masons, and perhaps begun 900 years earlier by King Solomon. Sealed off by the Turks in the 16th Century, they were rediscovered only by accident in 1852.

A low tunnel dug by Jebusites more than 3,000 years ago leads away in to the dark interior of Mount Ophel from the underground spring of Gihon. Threatened by Assyrian conquest in the 8th Century B.C., King Hezekiah had the tunnel extended to carry Jerusalem's water supply from outside the walls into the city.

To explore these strange waters, I stripped to my pants and plunged into the grotto. Then I followed the current into the jagged Jebusite tunnel. My candle guttered on sudden draughts. Soon I passed the shaft by which David had taken the city, 3,000 years before, and found myself in a later passageway that sliced boldly through the rock. The water ran gently around my waist, and under my bare feet the floor became smooth. The walls were no longer hacked with Jebusite roughness, but cut in the long, confident strokes of men who had the use of iron. They showed white and serried in my candlelight.

The two gangs of King Hezekiah's workmen, cutting their way towards each other under the threat of the Assyrian attack, had heard midway in the tunnel the sounds of each other's progress through the rock; and I could see where they had tried to meet. Near the end of the tunnel an inscription was found on its wall in a beautiful classical Hebrew: "Behold the Excavation! While the workmen were still lifting up the pick, each towards his comrade . . . a voice was heard of a man calling his fellow, since there was a split in the rock on the right hand and on the left. And on the day of the excavation the workmen struck, each towards his neighbour, pick against pick, and the water flowed from the spring to the pool for twelve hundred cubits, and a hundred cubits was the height of the rock above the head of the workmen." With the spring waters channelled into the city, and the wells outside blocked up, the Assyrian siege languished. Either disease or rebellion caused Sennacherib to march back to Nineveh, where years later his sons murdered him.

For a third of a mile Hezekiah's great conduit winds in an S-bend under the hill. Sometimes, where the stone was hard to cut and the workmen tired, the ceiling dips so low that there was barely room for my head above the waters. In these cramped quarters my candle was snuffed out and I stood in utter blackness, listening. The water purled faintly round my waist. There were muffled echoes, as if some creature was trapped behind the rock; and five minutes later, far ahead of me and isolated in their candle-light, I saw two young Jews groping in the same direction. The walls around them glowed remotely as they went, silhouetting their naked backs and shedding a long, wavering light over the water.

While still far under the hill, we heard the muezzin calling to prayer from a mosque above. A little farther, and a misty light spread over the walls ahead. I splashed out into dazzling sun shining on a quiet pool. It was to these "waters of Siloam which go softly", that Jesus sent the man born blind to wash his eyes. Its healing properties are still remembered, for the Arabs call it the Spring of Consolation and believe that it wells upwards from Eden. But crueller traditions have also survived; it is said that women accused of adultery were brought here to drink, and that if they were guilty the waters killed them. But now the traditional has given way to the practical; house-wives wash their clothes among the shallows, and small boys paddle there.

South of this pool, and fed by its stream, the valley where Solomon made his gardens is still green. I turned away from it, climbed over the wasteland of Ophel, and walked among ruined walls. A young Arab approached me with a dish of ancient coins. They were corroded almost to nothing, although here and there an imaginative eye might discern a Jewish chalice or the dimly crowned head of a Roman emperor.

"I've got everybody here." He juggled the coins in my face. "This is Hadrian, and this Herod. And here's Nero. All you need is lemon juice."

"Lemon juice?"

"Yes. Rub a bit on and they'll come up like new. I swear it. Augustus . . . Saladin . . . they only need lemon juice."

I shook my head and walked away through the ruins again. Already in the century after Hezekiah Jerusalem was expanding over slopes to the west. From this time archaeologists have found numerous pagan figurines —fertility goddesses with ringleted hair and plump breasts—lasting wit-nesses of the city's infidelity to its God.

Retribution came out of Babylon. In 598 B.C. Nebuchadnezzar captured Jerusalem, enslaved many of the nobles and set up a puppet king, Zedekiah. Ten years later this king rebelled, and the Babylonians returned in force. After an 18-month siege, the city, with its Temple and royal palace, was burnt to the ground. The walls were levelled and the bulk of the people led captive to Babylon. On the slopes of Ophel you may still see remnants of houses crushed under terraces that collapsed on them from above. A pair of plinths lies tumbled among thistles; some steps lead to a vanished door. There is nothing else. But the lament of Jerusalem's people, dying in exile, has become a heritage of the world:

The upturned palm of this blind man, one of Jerusalem's many beggars, is an invitation for the Muslim devout to perform their religious duty of almsgiving. Many on their way to work automatically drop coins into waiting hands.

By the waters of Babylon, there we sat down, yea,
we wept, when we remembered Zion. . . .
If I forget thee, O Jerusalem, let my right hand forget her
cunning.
If I do not remember thee, let my tongue cleave to the roof
of my mouth; if I prefer not Jerusalem above my chief joy.

It was usual for exiled peoples to respect the gods of those who had vanquished them—for these gods had proved stronger than their own—and to relinquish their beliefs for those of their conquerors. But to the Israelites the Babylonian deities were nothing—myths, merely, of sky and earth. Their own God had instilled in them too deep a conscience to be forsaken, and if Babylon had defeated them it was only as the instrument of His punishment. So the Israelites turned in on their own tradition, and survived. Jerusalem, lying in ruins, became the symbol both of God and nation; and when a kindlier power than Babylon—the conquering Cyrus of Persia—allowed the Jews to return, in 539 B.C., a chastened people began to trickle back. The Temple rose again, more modestly, on its mount, although the Ark had vanished. Years afterwards the governor Nehemiah rebuilt the city's walls on the crest of Ophel, leaving its older ruins smothered under the hill, where archaeologists were to find them more than two millennia later.

An unaccustomed peace settled on the city. It seemed as if the age of both suffering and inspiration had finally ended. For 200 years scholars and scribes expounded the great Law—the first five books of the Bible. In this quiet present the past became sacred.

It is said, too, that the Jews brought back Persian ideas from their exile—a new enquiry, a looking beyond the grave. Now the people turned to the study of their faith with an exclusive passion; they did not even allow pagans to live in Jerusalem. And so were laid the foundations of orthodox Judaism.

It was while wandering across Ophel that I fell in with a rabbi, and asked him about this inhospitality in the Jewish religion. "Judaism cannot be a truth for everyone," he answered, fixing me with a pair of frank but hesitant eyes. "We do not believe, as a Christian may, that a man is banned from paradise because he holds this or that faith. No. We believe rather in a basic religious standard." His arms outspread. "This we call 'the religion of the sons of Noah'—of all mankind. So Judaism is not the only way by which man can reach God. It is simply our way."

"But your way is better?" I fumbled. "Closer to truth?"

He smiled: an ugly, charming face. Red hair straggled under his skull cap and mingled with a red beard, as if his features were lapped in desultory flames. At their centre his eyes were full of waiting and appraisal. "It is rather as if mankind were a pattern of circles, one inside the other," he said. "At its core—yes—are the Jews, but this is more of a responsibility than anything. Because God has called us to be the world's priests—'And you

**A mason dresses a new block of local limestone.**

# History Built of Stone

The colour of Jerusalem, humble houses and grandiose monuments alike, is the colour of its local limestone. Herodian, Byzantine, Crusader and Turkish masonry, weathered to honey, grey-green or gold, forms a patchwork, the stones of one period often used again in the next. Their variety is suggested in this photographic mosaic. Many bear religious symbols, others display purely decorative motifs. The crosses second from right in the top row are in the Armenian quarter; the star of David (bottom row) graces the Hurva synagogue. The Arabic script at top left is from a 15th-Century Mameluke fountain, and the lion next to it is one of four marking the Lion Gate in the great city walls. The old harmony is preserved today by a regulation that requires the use of native limestone for all repairs and any new building, to safeguard the city's character.

will be unto me a kingdom of priests and a holy nation.' That is both our privilege and burden. There's no need for others to envy us. What we are born to makes no difference in the soul. It is like men and women—why should one be like the other?"

His view—Judaism produces many views but no dogma—warmed me to the rabbi, but I asked how this nation of priests thought to influence the world if it had no missionary impetus.

The rabbi pulled a charred pipe out of his pocket, but did not light it. "A priest's duty"—his voice was high and gentle—"is first to give Mass, only second to preach a sermon. Isn't that so in Christianity? And it's the same with us. By our presence, if it is good, we can unite the world with God."

"But that is not your purpose?"

"Not precisely. We exist for God, not man. When a candle burns, its purpose is not to illuminate; it burns for itself. Yet it sheds light all around." He lit his pipe, as if for a symbol. "Yes, the secret is in the mere existence of a people devoted in such a way. They create a question-mark, a need to describe or explain. Their influence is, literally, incalculable." The rabbi rubbed back the damp locks of hair from his forehead and looked at me pleasantly. "It is the existence of a thing which matters. Not what it tries to teach, but what it is."

This sense of Israel as the Chosen, as a focus of God's intent, has always been interpreted practically. Judaism is still a religion more of ethic than of enquiry. And it still ignores the afterlife. "It's almost considered vulgar to talk of it!" The rabbi laughed. "After all, it adds nothing to spiritual conduct. The motives for goodness are love and fear of God. Nothing more. In childhood we may be bribed with sweets or threatened with a beating. But later we are rewarded by more elaborate things, until at last we come to love goodness for itself."

As he wandered among the fallen stones I saw how thin his arms were, but his stomach was unnaturally distended. Against this physical deformity, I guessed, his mind had flourished. "Our so-called enlightened men", he went on, "don't like to speak of the afterlife. The common people have always thought about it more than the rabbis have. It's almost a folk religion for them. All the same, in Judaism our hell is more like Dante's, a place from which all except a very few return."

But the Jews once associated a place on earth with hell. To the south of Old Jerusalem the walls are bounded by the deserted valley called Gehenna, and even today this glade is filled by evil memories and over-looked by peaks whose names spell corruption. In summer the olive trees, long abandoned, wilt on their crumbling terraces, and the scrub beneath is burnt to thorns. On one side, as you ascend the valley, looms the Mount of Scandal, where Solomon built an altar to the bloodstained god of Moab. On another, from a corner of the Temple that can still be seen, St. James, the brother of Christ, was thrown to his martyrdom. And to the left, on the

Mount of Evil Counsel, the Pharisees in legend plotted the death of Jesus.

This valley is still called Ge-Hinnom in Hebrew—the Valley of the Son of Hinnom, which contracted to "Gehenna". Here in the 7th Century B.C. children were sacrificed by fire inside the brazen belly of the god Moloch, while priests beat drums to drown out their screaming. One of the kings of Judah gave his own son to be burnt. Even after the cult was destroyed some horror lingered in the place. No more, warned the Book of Jeremiah, should the place be called the Valley of the Son of Hinnom, but the valley of slaughter: and the people would bury their dead there, until it overflowed. "And the carcasses of this people shall be meat for the fowls of the heaven, and for the beasts of the earth; and none shall fright them away." In the time of Christ it was covered by a stench of smoke, for it had become the city's refuse-tip, and at night the fires flickered along its gully.

The valley is riddled with ancient graves. In early Christian years, after the corpses had decomposed, hermits and anchorites inhabited the tombs, but a tale has it that they were massacred on a mistaken order, and buried where they had lived. Later still, the bodies of medieval pilgrims, dying far from home, were laid there unremembered.

Many an unpleasant biblical site was relegated to Gehenna. Here used to be shown the tree from which Judas hanged himself, as well as the field purchased by the priests with the blood money that he returned to them: 30 shekels of silver. For the priests "took counsel, and bought with them the potter's field, to bury strangers in. Wherefore that field was called the field of blood, unto this day."

A no-man's-land between Israel and Jordan until the 1967 war, the valley is now a wasteland of thistles, for which a man would scarcely sell his sandals, let alone his God. But in keeping with the charity of burying strangers here, the Crusaders built a charnel-house. Its vaults rise 60 feet into the air and are pierced with holes through which the corpses of pilgrims were thrown. But even this mortuary, it seems, was insufficient, and travellers wrote of bodies laid in the valley unburied, so that Jeremiah's prophecy was fulfilled and it became a haunt of jackals and vultures. Pilgrims, in fact, were the perennial sufferers in the Holy Land, and Jerusalem especially was hard on those who came there. In the face of disease, murder and extortion, many of those who sought out the City of Heaven on earth ended as dust in its Gehenna.

# A Wall of Grief and Joy

**Written prayers tucked into crevices in the stones of the Wall are thought by those who place them there to carry their messages straight to God.**

In the south-east section of the Old City rises the sheer 58-foot cliff of the Wailing Wall, or Western Wall, as it is sometimes called—holiest of holy places for religious Jews throughout the world. Historically it is a section of the retaining wall that King Herod had constructed of massive limestone blocks when he enlarged the site of King Solomon's Temple to accommodate his own majestic new Temple.

In A.D. 70 the Romans attacked Jerusalem, destroyed Herod's Temple and drove the surviving Jews into exile. But the solid masonry of the Temple's substructure survived and the Wall has stood through successive centuries more or less unchanged. To the exiled Jews it soon became a focus of their longing and a goal for their pilgrimage, a symbolic fragment of the ancient Temple and of the Jerusalem that they had lost.

In the heat of afternoon, the broad plaza before the Wailing Wall is deserted although worshippers cluster at the Wall itself. The open space dates from after the Six-Day War of 1967, when the crowded houses of the Moroccan quarter were demolished to make way for the paved plaza. Above the Wall and to the left is the golden Dome of the Rock, and at the far right gleams the silver dome of the Aqsa Mosque, another focus of Muslim veneration and worship.

A Hasidic Jew prays leaning against the Wall.

An elderly man rests his prayer-book in a niche.

Studying prayers, a young Jew in a beaver hat shades his eyes from light reflected by the stones.

# The Passion of Prayer

The devout Jew feels God's presence close when he prays alone at the Wailing Wall, face turned to the ancient stones. At such a moment and in such a hallowed place no rabbi is required to mediate his colloquy with God. Thus the Wall serves its benign purpose, whether for a Hasid or orthodox pietist, the less formal visit of a plain citizen, or the once-in-a-lifetime pilgrimage of a non-Israeli Jew.

Father and son worshipping at the Wall share a fringed prayer-shawl, the son drawing it over his father's head in a moving gesture of reverence and devotion.

After finishing their service one group starts a joyful dance while others still pray at the Wall. The woven screen separates the men from the women (at top).

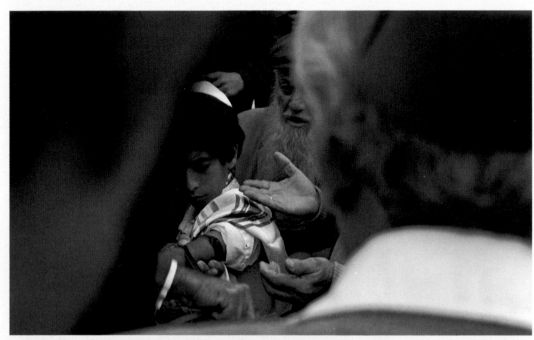

**At the Wall, adults fasten straps holding a phylactery (a prayer box) to a boy's arm during a bar mitzvah.**

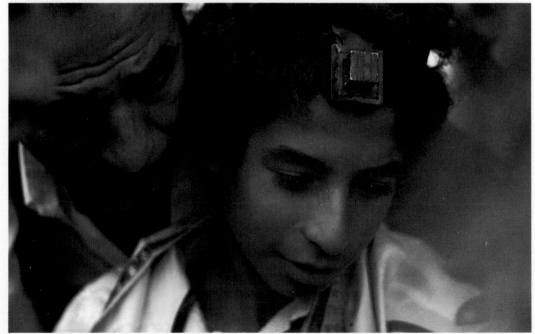

**Awed by the rite, the 13-year-old wears on his brow a phylactery containing Old Testament verses.**

## Ceremonies of Exaltation

Jews come to the Wall for important occasions, both those of the communal religious year and those of the individual's religious life. The joyful celebration at left marks the Festival of the Law that ends the Feast of Tabernacles, one of three great annual festivals. The *bar mitzvah* (above) is the most important event of a Jewish boy's life, representing his initiation into the religious community—and manhood.

At a night-time swearing-in ceremony the burning insignia of Israeli paratroopers casts an orange glow on the floodlit Wall. All Israeli paratroopers—members of the elite force that regained possession of the Wall from the Jordanians in 1967—are sworn in here. They pledge themselves at this relic of Herod's Temple to protect the new "temple"—today's state of Israel—from any foe.

# 3

# The Yoke of Greece and Rome

"Ten measures of suffering", runs a Hebrew myth, "were sent by God upon the world—and nine of them fell on Jerusalem." And it is true; no city has been ravaged more terribly. The peace that settled on Jerusalem after the return of the Jews from their Babylonian exile was only temporary. The arrival of Greeks in the 4th Century B.C. heralded a period of unequalled savagery. So deep went these disasters, culminating four centuries later in the Roman sack of the city and the expulsion yet again of the Jews, that Jerusalem was changed forever. In my wanderings through the city, I was to find that scarcely one stone rested where it had during the Old and New Testament past—the very skeleton of the present-day streets was shaped not by the Jews, but by the Romans.

This tragic conflict between East and West began long ago in 332 B.C., when the Persian Empire was overturned by Alexander the Great. Nine years later, the young conqueror died in Babylon, and his dominions were split among his followers. Jerusalem fell to the lot of the Greek kings of Egypt and for a while the city was fortunate. The kings dealt so leniently with Judea that its people virtually governed themselves. But a century later the province was absorbed by the Seleucids of Syria—Greek rulers with a missionary desire to unite Asia under Hellenism. Antiochus IV, who bore the modest title "God Made Manifest", built a theatre, amphitheatre and gymnasium in the city. The influence of the new culture spread rapidly, and many Jews took to wearing Greek dress and affecting Greek manners and speech. Within sight of the Temple they ran naked in the gymnasium—or nearly naked, for out of shame, wrote the Jewish historian Josephus, they concealed their circumcision.

Yet no two minds could have differed more profoundly than those of Greek and Jew. Their opposing streams—Semitic faith and Hellenic reason—have permeated all the centuries of Western history. The Greek gods were little better than ordinary men, and sometimes worse. Capricious or indifferent, they could not curb the flexible intelligence of their people, who loved the world and enquired into its essence. The true self of man, wrote Aristotle, was Reason.

But to the Jews these strange and versatile people were engaged in a blasphemous quest for something both impossible and unnecessary. The nature of the world was unknowable. "My thoughts", God had said, "are not your thoughts, neither are your ways my ways." The human duty was not enquiry but obedience. To the Jews such obedience was the life of the soul, to the Greeks the death of the mind.

Carved from the cliff that now encloses it, the Tomb of Zachariah (it is in fact a funerary monument to a priestly family) dates from the 3rd or 2nd Century B.C. when Greeks held sway over Jerusalem. Behind it are the more recent graves of Jews, and at its base is a pit dug in 1961 by archaeologists searching for treasure believed to have been buried there in the 1st Century A.D. by Jews fleeing Roman persecution.

In 167 B.C. Antiochus—who seems to have made a speciality of sacking shrines—marched a garrison into Jerusalem and abolished its worship. Greek ritual was enforced by arms, and in the Temple itself was placed that "abomination of desolation", the idol of Olympian Zeus. Now the sterner Jews rebelled. For 25 years, led by the family of Judas Maccabaeus, they fought for their God. When at last they triumphed, they set up their own dynasty of priest-kings—who grew secular and corrupt in their turn.

But in any case, it was a poor brand of Hellenism that blossomed and then withered in Jerusalem—a showy and slightly effete culture. You may see it even now, scattered around the city in rock-cut tombs whose odd blend of the classical and the oriental has a gloomy fascination. Down in the King's Dale, opposite Ophel, the cenotaphs rise in weird cones and pyramids. One of them was for centuries mistaken for the tomb of Absalom, David's disloyal son, and passers-by of all three religions are said to have hurled rocks at it, shouting insults, until a hole was battered in its side.

Also preserved is a lovelier sepulchre, to the north of the walled city; it is that of Queen Helen of Adiaben, a Jewish convert from Mesopotamia. A monumental staircase, cut 30 feet wide in virgin rock, descends to a courtyard and to the sepulchre's palatial entranceway. Above it a frieze of grapes and garlands has faded to a ghost in the rock. Beneath, a stone is rolled away from a tiny opening. Here in a secret chamber a 19th-Century archaeologist, believing he had found the necropolis of the biblical kings, opened the royal sarcophagus. For a moment he saw the queen lying with her arms crossed on her breast, perfectly preserved in the airless vault. Then she crumbled away before his eyes, leaving among dust and bones only the gold threads of her shroud.

None of the large buildings of this period survives, and little more than its scattering of tombs is left at all. But while the last Maccabean kings were struggling over the succession, a greater power than any before was thrusting its way south—a power that was to mark the character of Jerusalem even to the present day. It was a force that overcame its enemies not by the seductive grace of its culture, as had Hellenism, but by the disciplined might of its legions. In 63 B.C., the year of Cicero's consulship and Augustus's birth, the Roman general Pompey, marching out of a beaten Armenia, exploited the troubles of the rulers in Judea to move against Jerusalem. After a three-month siege, his soldiers broke into the Temple, cutting down the priests as they continued the rites of sacrifice to the last.

Such a violation symbolized all that was to come between the Jews and Romans. The Jews could not bend; the Romans could not understand. But the Romans for a time preferred to rule through others—above all, the shrewd and capable family of Herod the Great. This extraordinary man, who degenerated from a brilliant and subtle ruler into a vindictive maniac, has set his seal on Jerusalem more profoundly than any other monarch. A loyal servant of Rome, who retained even Mark Antony's friendship—despite the hatred of Cleopatra—Herod came of the Idumean Arab nation, which was Jewish by adoption. And the lot of his people, although they loathed him personally, was rarely better than during the 34 years in which he reigned in Jerusalem.

So little did the Jews trust him that when Herod proclaimed his intent to rebuild the Temple, they suspected him of wishing to dedicate it to Augustus Caesar. Nevertheless, the titanic building project—the historian Josephus called it "the most prodigious work that was ever heard of by man"—was started in 19 B.C., and was all but finished 18 years later. A thousand priests were trained as masons and carpenters so that no unclean hand would defile its inner sanctuary. Above the City of David, the cliffs were hacked sheer in the north; and to the south the falling slopes were shored up on a thicket of subterranean arches. Over 35 acres, this great paved hill was bounded by deep colonnades. Each interlocking court rose upon the last in a dazzling mountain of stone, increasing in sanctity as the worshipper penetrated its awesome gateways.

High above all, its golden porch glistening 150 feet in the air, the holy sanctuary kept to the sacred proportions of Solomon's model. Not even birds violated it; they were kept away by gilded spikes covering the roof. Every day, from the altar at its steps, an ancient ritual—the sounds of high, Levite chant, of harp and cymbal—mixed with the bellowing of animals led to slaughter, the stench of fly-covered entrails, blood and burning flesh. But the shrine's interior was narrow and dim, filled with the smoke of the great seven-branched *menorah* and heavy with the mingled smells of incense and sacrifice. Only the High Priest could penetrate, once a year, into the emptiness at its heart, the Holy of Holies.

The finished Temple lasted only six years—until the Romans under Titus levelled it in a siege of unsurpassed horror. Yet even today the colossal platform on which it stood, crowned by the Dome of the Rock, is the most powerful feature of the city, occupying one-sixth of the walled town. To south and east, high above the Kidron valley, the Ottoman conquerors in the 16th Century built their ramparts upon the Temple walls; its stones still burgeon from the ground, sometimes so worn that they are compacted together like living rock, sometimes appearing as smooth as when they were first cut. These great blocks, rising and dipping in the waves of the earth, go astonishingly deep. In the 19th Century, Captain Charles Warren, a British engineer, sank shafts beside the wall; at times he had to send them down 80 or 100 feet before reaching bedrock, where the hill itself had been notched to receive the stones.

Where I walked above them, Muslim tombs were crumbling in the sun. Among them the graves of the poor were traced by circles of stones—the tombs of the rich rose taller in a vain inequality of death. I stumbled upon an old man sleeping among the tombs. He reproached me in a whisper.

From the far side of the valley I could hear the cries of Jewish mourners over their graves; their lamentation fell on the air with a lonely sorrow. I turned by the Temple's south-east angle and saw the courses of its wall rearing 80 feet into the air. This, perhaps, was the pinnacle of the Temple— from which Satan, says the New Testament, tempted Jesus to cast himself down. The wall plunges almost as deep beneath the ground as it stands above it, and I remembered the words of the awestruck apostles to their master: "See what manner of stones and what buildings are here!"

Along the southern limit of Herod's Temple the Royal Portico ran for more than 900 yards, lifting in two tiers 100 feet into the sky. Underneath it burrowed the "Gates of the Mole", double and triple passageways that Jewish legend said would survive the ruin of the Temple. And so they have. The Muslims have locked them now, but a gentle bribe will gain access, and it was almost with fear that I found myself walking there. The only light filtered in from the entranceways. My footprints went deep in years of dust. On either hand the monolithic pillars rose colourless, as if in twilight. They stood as Josephus described them, so thick "that three men might, with their arms extended, fathom it around". In the dry vault I could hear my breath come faster. Such sites are rare in Jerusalem or have been replaced by frauds—the traveller is always being urged into a portentous grotto or shrine. But now and then, with this strange quickening of the heart, he finds himself in some half-ignored place, whose legends are true. These moments touch him with a sudden awe. He sees indelible in rock, as I did, the uncertainty of Hezekiah's tunnellers as they groped to meet; or he stands in the spring where Solomon was anointed. Now, touching these gaunt columns, I realized that the passage in which I stood had been trodden by Christ, Mary, St. Paul. There could be no doubt, either, about the sanctity of the terrace and the wide steps excavated beyond it. Every saint of the New Testament must have climbed them.

There are other gates into the Temple precincts, too—all named, rather absurdly, after the English or American gentlemen who first located them. I left the dark of the Mole Gates for the sunlight outside, then crept into the shadows again under Wilson's Arch, whose causeway linked the Temple to the upper city. Ever since the Six-Day War, pious Jews have been carrying on excavations here, because it adjoins the Wailing Wall. Nowhere in Jerusalem can you see better the depth and complexity of the city than in these excavations—age after age heaped on itself for more than 60 feet down. Here in the last century Captain Warren broke into a subterranean gallery of unknown antiquity, which extended for 250 feet under the road. He followed a maze of chambers and passageways, finally emerging covered in dirt at the back of a donkey stable, whose owner bolted in terror, shouting that genii were after him.

Beneath the vaults near the Wailing Wall I found Hasidic Jews, seated on benches, swaying to the rhythm of their prayer. Under their hats their eyes

RICHARD CLEAVE

A model of Herod's Jerusalem, complete with Herod's Temple (above and top left of the large picture), occupies grounds of the Holyland Hotel. The structure with towers is the Antonia Fortress, while to the far right of it, just outside the wall, is Golgotha, the Place of the Skull, where tradition places Jesus's crucifixion. Behind the fortress a broad rampart forms the structure that partially survives today as the Wailing Wall.

were kindly but abstract, and in their beards the pale lips seemed to murmur of a timeless loss. Near by I fell into conversation with a Jew who professed belief in Christ. His sprightly black eyes fixed me from under the rim of a straw hat. Jesus, he said, was the Messiah, but the Christian Church had shrouded him in dogma and had persecuted his people, the Jews. "But I tell you he is coming, the Messiah is coming again." He tugged a button off his shirtfront in his urgency. "Yes, very soon now. Isn't it written that when Israel returns to Jerusalem he will come? There is the hand of God in this." From the sunlight outside the vaults, where boys were being ceremonially initiated into manhood against the Wailing Wall, came the muffled shouts of people rejoicing.

"You believe the Messiah will come in your lifetime?" My voice sounded ridiculously matter-of-fact.

"Yes, yes. Within ten years. It's close, it's coming." Then he touched my arm in warning: "But first the Anti-Christ will appear. Yes, a world ruler will arise, a monster who will demand worship." He lifted up his hands. " . . . But Christ will come in his glory—and the Temple be built again!"

I asked: "Why Christ?"

He leaned for a moment against the huge courses of stones that surrounded us. "When the Romans destroyed the Temple," he said, "the Jews could no longer sacrifice. We could not atone properly for sin. Sacrifice, you see, was only lawful in the Temple. So God sent Christ instead—and the crucifixion was our blood sacrifice and atonement!"

This curious synthesis of Judaism and Christianity—it has a small following in Israel—had brought this Jew to the Church of the Holy Sepulchre, where he had prayed by the tomb of Jesus. And later I saw him among many others of his people murmuring and kissing the Wall, his small frame frail against its monumental stones.

If you walk now on the platform where the Temple stood, you see the Dome of the Rock, set on its summit in startling beauty. Yet all about it the emptiness is coldly eloquent. Nothing can fill it: not the few orchards and gardens, not the dry fountains. The ghost of Herod's building is everywhere. In the south-east, and deep under the pavements, the Muslims—who call Christ the second among prophets—venerate a shrine as the place where the Virgin Mary hid with her child on their flight to Egypt. And beneath it again, in the so-called Stables of Solomon, spreads a stagnant forest of 88 colossal Herodian piers, supporting the esplanade of the vanished Temple above; here, in the 12th Century, the Crusaders quartered their camels and horses.

In Herod's time Jerusalem was a city of formidable strength; since the Jewish return from Babylon it had spread far over its western hill. And within 60 years of Herod's death its walls had driven north to the line that they follow today—perhaps farther. An old aqueduct, carrying water from pools beyond Bethlehem, had fed the city for centuries. Pontius Pilate was

Survivors of Herod's day, the Stables of Solomon were misnamed by the Crusaders who kept their horses here. The piers and vaults still support a broad esplanade, once part of Herod's grandiose Temple complex.

soon to build a new one, cutting over the landscape in ruthless Roman fashion. The timeless cisterns that were fed by these waterways are still sunk in the city, fetid in winter and empty in summer.

Herod channelled the flow into the gardens of his palace-citadel, where statues stood among the pools and the trees were filled with doves. Surrounded by ramparts from which his mercenaries could watch the streets, the suspicious king held a court of oriental splendour. Josephus writes that here Herod raised three towers "for largeness, beauty, and strength, beyond all that were in the habitable earth", and named the first two in memory of his dead brother, Phasael, and his dead friend, Hippicus. The third, more delicate and luxurious, he called after Mariamne, his second wife, a beautiful Jewess of the royal Maccabean dynasty. These three bastions, with their interknit walls, became the strength of a fortress which alone survived the Roman siege of A.D. 70. Every power thereafter—Byzantine, Arab, Crusader—fenced the castle anew. And now, high in the city's west, it encloses a tangle of overgrown excavations.

The towers of Mariamne and Hippicus are gone, but beneath the castle's keep, lifting from the tired earth in 15 layers of stone, the bastion of Phasael squats like a titan in the sun. Such stones were Herod's defence. He trusted nobody, and he was right. As his reign continued, it sank in blood. His suspicion grew close to madness. On a groundless charge of infidelity he executed Mariamne, and then fell into demented weeping when she was gone; for months he ordered his servants to call to her as if she were still alive. From liquidating more than half of the Jewish supreme council, and uncounted subjects, Herod went on to order the stoning of 300 army officers, the strangling of his two sons and the execution—while he was on his own deathbed—of a third. Josephus writes that Herod was diseased, and has given so detailed and revolting a description of his malady that modern doctors have attributed his persecution mania to combined afflictions of sclerosis and gangrene. Little wonder that such a king inspired the legend of the slaughter of infants at Bethlehem.

Walking by this all-but-vanished palace, whose couches might seat 200 foreign guests, I could understand why the Jews hated this foreign king whose master was Rome. Many of his soldiers, even, were German and Idumean mercenaries, with a regiment of Galatians who had once been the bodyguard of Cleopatra.

Now the great bossed stones of the Phasael make all else seem light around them. Lizards flicker in the weeds beneath. As Herod grew old, he could no longer climb these towers with their sad names, but had to be carried in a litter. He died at last in 4 B.C., to be buried in his mountain tomb between the desert and Bethlehem.

No city on earth can have suffered more numerous or atrocious sieges than Jerusalem, and the most significant of these, as well as the most terrible, was now drawing near. The city had been harshly governed. Herod's

Bargaining traders inspect their long-eared sheep.

An Arab girl, incongruously clad in a gold lamé dress, keeps attentive watch over her father's flock.

## Ancient Sheep Market

Against the north-east city wall where ancient graveyards dot the slopes, a sheep market takes place each Friday. Just how long it has been going on no one knows, but in biblical times shepherds brought sacrificial sheep to the Pool of Bethesda close by.

From the surrounding hills the shepherds still bring in their animals before dawn, and by first light the market is already busy as men bargain to supplement their breeding stock or increase their flocks. Buyers lead their purchases away through the long shadows cast by the rising sun, and by 10 or 11 a.m. the market place is quiet again.

At sunrise, newly-bought sheep, led by goats and followed by their owner, head home along a road that winds through a crowded Muslim graveyard.

death removed the last effective buffer between Roman boorishness and Jewish intransigence. From A.D. 6 until A.D. 66, apart from the three-year reign of Herod Agrippa, Judea was ruled by a succession of venal and contemptuous procurators, of whom Pontius Pilate was typical. But in 66 the oppressed Jews broke into open revolt and slew the Roman garrison in Jerusalem. The legate of Syria, marching too slowly south, was beaten back with heavy losses. All Judea rose in arms, and in half of the eastern cities of the Empire pagans and Jews slaughtered one another.

Rome moved with slow but heavy purpose. Three of her finest legions— 70,000 veterans—were placed under the command of Vespasian, a Sabine peasant who had risen from the ranks in the reign of Claudius and had fought in the West Country of England. Moving south, he methodically overran Galilee, capturing its commander, the historian Josephus, who went over to the Romans and witnessed the war from their side. As Vespasian advanced down the Jordan valley, the solitary order of Essenes, taking flight, hid its sacred scrolls in the caves of the Dead Sea—to astonish the world nearly 1,900 years later. At the same time, the Christians—a heretical Jewish sect in its infancy—fled from the city and took refuge over the Jordan, perhaps remembering the warning of their founder that "Jerusalem shall be trodden down of the Gentiles". By A.D. 69 the city was surrounded and alone. And the Jews inside were not united: three different factions were struggling with each other for dominance.

In Rome, Nero had committed suicide and two stop-gap emperors had come and gone. Early the next year, proclaimed by his Egyptian legions, Vespasian sailed westward to assume the purple, leaving the assault on Jerusalem to his 30-year-old son Titus.

In the spring of A.D. 70, at the time of Passover, Titus appeared before the city and spread his camps on three sides. Later the Jews were to remember many portents. On the night of that Passover the earth shook and the doors of the Temple swung open of their own accord, while a ghostly concourse was heard passing through them, calling to one another to depart.

Within the city, the war for dominance had been raging intermittently for three years, and even now it continued—the factions murdering one another from their strongholds in different quarters. Titus attacked with battering rams from the north-west, and captured the outer ramparts by early May. Two weeks later, after bitter fighting, he took the second wall. The Jews retreated into the inner fortified city, with its Temple and the formidable Antonia fortress that Herod had named in honour of Mark Antony. Titus, daunted by so embattled a place, settled down to starve it out.

Now the true horror began: "Famine", Josephus wrote, "indeed overpowers all the emotions." The people died in their homes or while wandering the streets, and were too sick even to bury the dead. Some slipped outside the walls, desperately searching for grass or herbs; those who were captured were crucified in grotesque postures, sometimes as many as 500

In a new use for the past, the stump of a Roman column serves as the base of a street lamp. The Latin inscription reads in part: "To Marcus Junius Maximus, Legate of the Emperors in command of the 10th Legion". The column is one of the few visible reminders in Jerusalem of the Emperor Hadrian's city, Aelia Capitolina, laid out by him in the 2nd Century A.D.

a day, until there was no more room on the ramparts for the forest of their crosses. When the Arab mercenaries of the Romans discovered that a few of their captives had concealed gold coins by swallowing them, they slit open the stomachs of 2,000 in a single night.

But the Jews still held the Romans at the last walls, and it was not until late July, and by stealth, that the Antonia was taken. By now Jerusalem was a city of the dead. Josephus, quoting one of the gatekeepers, wrote that 115,000 corpses were carried out through that way alone. Inside the walls the soldiers were gnawing their leather shields and sandals, and a mother roasted and ate her own child—so that Titus, on hearing it, swore that he "would not leave upon the face of the earth, for the sun to behold, a city in which mothers were thus fed."

The Romans battled a month for the Temple, finally firing its gates and entering the outer court. Titus had given orders that the sanctuary be spared. But by the time the assault had been carried to the inner courts, his soldiers were out of control, and one of them "cast fire on the gate's hinges in the dark, so that the flames leapt out from the holy house, and Caesar and the generals retired, and no one any longer forbade its burning; and thus was the holy house destroyed, without Caesar's assent."

Titus completed the devastation. He ordered the city to be razed to the ground. Only the great towers of Herod and a part of the western rampart were preserved, as a camp for the legion that remained in the ruins, and as a token of the glory that the Romans had overcome.

Sixty years later, travelling his empire on foot and finding the great capital still desolate, the Emperor Hadrian, who loved all things Greek, decided to build on its site a pure Hellenistic city. Those Jews who remained again revolted. For three and a half years, under the fanatic leadership of Bar Kochba, "Son of a Star", they held out from Jerusalem and from a nest of lairs and strongholds in the desert hills. But the Roman retribution was pitiless. By A.D. 135, the last of them was annihilated, and in the markets of the East the Jewish slave became so common that he was sold for the price of a horse.

Meanwhile, Hadrian built his new Jerusalem. He levelled the ruins, even ploughed over them; and upon the slopes he set the city of Aelia Capitolina, whose name is remembered in the casual Arab *Ilya* of today. Compact, geometric, this metropolis staked out its limits along the lines that the Turkish walls still follow. To the south the ancient town of David on Ophel was excluded, and over the ruins of the Temple the emperor set up statues to Jupiter and himself. He carved his streets with classical precision, burying the older city under his beautiful and sterile colonnades.

Walking to-day down the arteries of the Old City—the Street of the Chain, El-Wad, the Khan es-Zeit—you may see that for all the tumult of their shops they move with a needle straightness. Here and there, leaning out of walls or absorbed into them, the trunks of half-buried columns poke up in sad ambiguity. I noticed one enclosed in a Christian shrine, another supporting an arch; the smooth head of yet another had been used by the near-by butcher as a chopping block; it trickled blood.

Now Aelia Capitolina is itself in fragments. A Russian convent encloses an arch of its forum; the monument at its crossroads supports an Arab café. Strangest of all, the gate that was believed since medieval times to be the one beneath which Jesus was condemned turns out instead to be part of Hadrian's eastern entrance. But this discovery came too late. The Sisters of Zion, a businesslike order of nuns, had already enclosed it in a church. And there it is still. The sisters cheerfully accept their mistake and attend Mass every morning before the gate of the pagan emperor. In their clinical shrine it sheds a tired lustre, as if abandoned.

For two centuries after A.D. 135 no Jew was allowed within sight of the city, on pain of death. A community of Gentile Christians grew up on the western hill, now called Mount Zion, but they no longer observed the Jewish traditions of the Church's infancy, and even their liturgy was sung in Greek. The Romans transferred the capital to Caesarea on the coast, and Aelia Capitolina became a backwater.

As for the Jews, they were scattered by now over all the known world. Unique among peoples, they endured because their sacred scriptures held them together with laws deeper and more intimate than any they encountered. Thus was created a ritualism that separated them from others. Often it declined into mere habit; but its essence was a contact between man and God in the simple routine of life. Because of this—and because they were shunned or persecuted as murderers of Jesus—the Jews survived.

But they were forever homesick. Year after year, century after century, the final blessing of Passover ended with the anguished call: "Next year in Jerusalem". All synagogues were oriented to the city. A Jerusalem of legendary beauty grew in the people's minds. This paradise on earth was unsullied by the stench of death—even of flowers—and disease was unknown. No fire broke out, no home collapsed in this dream city. "The world is like unto the human eye," said the sages, "for the white is the ocean which girds the earth; the iris is the earth upon which we dwell; the pupil is Jerusalem and the image therein is the Temple of the Lord." So closely woven were place and people that Jerusalem was regarded almost as sentient, a city to be comforted, healed and petitioned. To be buried beside its walls was to lie beneath the throne of God.

Yet there were contrary, sadder traditions. It was said that ever since the Temple's destruction, men of wisdom had vanished from the nation, that in Jerusalem the rains and dew had dried up and the trees stood barren around a city no longer pure.

The emperor Constantine, early in the 4th Century A.D., permitted Jews to return only once a year. A pilgrim records them visiting the site of the Temple: "a perforated stone which they anoint, then lament with groans and tear their robes and depart". By the end of the 5th Century the place was again forbidden them entirely; but in 638 the Muslims, whose newly-founded religion shared in Jewish traditions, captured and reconsecrated the site. And by medieval times, a small community of Jews was generally to be found in the upper town.

But Jewish pilgrims found their city smothered by the buildings and the faiths of other men. As they approached, they cried out, according to formula: "Zion is a wilderness, Jerusalem a desolation," and rent their garments, then tore them again upon sight of the Temple. "The formality should be carried out standing," said the rabbis, "It should be done with the hand; the rents should be extended until the heart is laid bare; and they must never be sewed up again."

And who shall grant me, on the wings of eagles,
To rise and seek thee through the years,
Until I mingle with thy dust beloved,
The waters of my tears?
Shall I not to thy very stones be tender?
Shall I not kiss them verily?
Shall not thine earth upon my lips taste sweeter
Than honey unto me?

This was the medieval poet-pilgrim Halevi, who travelled to Jerusalem from Spain, and was trampled to death by an Arab horseman (runs the tale) as he knelt in the dust of the city.

Yet there were some Jews, soon after the destruction of the Temple, who had the vision not to count it pure loss. One rabbi even wrote boldly that a great wall had been demolished between God and His chosen people. For now the entire system of burnt offering became obsolete, and henceforth sacrifice would be made in the heart.

# 4

# The Presence of Christ

For the Christian, a visit to Jerusalem is a trial of faith, and his reaction to the city is often a violent one. Following the footprints of Christ among streets and shrines now devoted to commerce may be deeply distressing. Yet the feel of today's Jerusalem is startlingly like that of the capital in ferment that Jesus himself knew.

Since before medieval times the city has worked its fascination on both the simplest and most sophisticated pilgrims. To see the same landscape, to tread the earth where Divinity has walked, forges for the Christian a mystical link to God—a God who lived and suffered as a man.

The debate as to where, precisely, the events of Christ's Passion took place, has been a playground for every kind of mystic, scholar and bigot. For little survives from Christ's time. In the years after his Crucifixion the city was twice sacked and razed by Rome. The Bible itself is often unclear. Jesus, it seems, was captured, tried and crucified in a single night and day. He was betrayed by the kiss of Judas in the Garden of Gethsemane. He was led to trial before the Jewish high priesthood in mansions that probably stood in the upper city. And he was convicted by Pontius Pilate in one of the two great palace-forts whose ruins remain—either in Jerusalem's Citadel or in the Antonia Fortress adjoining the Temple. Finally he was led to his death outside the city walls at Golgotha, "place of a skull", and was buried near by in a tomb on a site unnamed.

Every moment of that suffering is now consecrated by some shrine or other, and if a person is to follow this route, as I was about to do, he will be happiest if he has either a strong faith, or none at all. I began by retracing Christ's movements in the final hours of his life—wandering from the traditional site of the Last Supper on Mount Zion through the Garden of Gethsemane on the Mount of Olives to the supposed scene of his betrayal by Peter on the morn of the Crucifixion.

The Crucifixion seems to have passed little noticed in its day. Jesus's followers in Jerusalem, a community of pious Jews, faded from record after the Roman sack in A.D. 70. But Paul had already carried his vision of Christ across the Mediterranean, and within a few decades Christianity had ceased to be a Jewish faction and become a gospel of world salvation.

Three hundred years after the Crucifixion the deeds of Holy Week began to be commemorated in stone. Pious men identified one spot after another with Christ and his suffering. The city fell in love with its victim. And today, still, it is the Galilean Jew, walking in a precise historical period, whose memory permeates the city more than that of any other man. In church,

Six bulbous domes poke into mist blanketing the grounds of the convent church of St. Mary Magdalene near the Garden of Gethsemane, scene of Christ's passion. Founded in 1885 by Czar Alexander III, the convent now houses a dwindling community of White Russian nuns.

cave and sanctuary, by Orthodox or Roman Catholic, Armenian and Copt, every speech and act of Christ's Passion is possessively enshrined.

The traditional site of the Upper Room, where the Last Supper took place, has been sanctified on Mount Zion since the 4th Century—perhaps earlier, for it was said that in the time of the Roman emperor Hadrian a group of Christians lived here in remembrance of Jesus. Successive churches have come and gone in its honour, and by medieval times its cult was so elaborate that pilgrims were even shown the grille where the Last Supper was cooked. But instead of an oriental chamber, I found an echoing Gothic hall built for the Franciscans by masons of the Cypriot Crusader kings. Over its flagstone floor the vaulting arched with a clear, solemn strength; and its caretaker, an old Arab with a quizzical face, could find nothing to point out—he only shivered slightly and wandered away.

After the Last Supper, say the Gospels, Jesus went with his disciples over the Kidron brook to the Garden of Gethsemane. As I descended Mount Zion I found myself on a stairway of worn, patinated stones, dropping among carob and pine trees. These steps were not the ones Jesus had trod, but they followed a way far older, going down to the Pool of Siloam. Such tracks, like streams, are scarcely changed by time, and the Kidron too, although thinned by irrigation, has left its scar in the valley east of Jerusalem.

Steep from this glade, where orchards mingle with the black crosses of Christian dead, the Mount of Olives rises to a battered summit, down which old footpaths trickle. This Mount is not a mountain at all, but a slope blending to other slopes, encrusted with shrines and legends. Nothing but a tough gorse rasped under my feet as I climbed it. To the north showed the silhouette of Mount Scopus, between 1948 and 1967 an Israeli enclave in Jordanian land, while down the southern slopes of the Mount itself poured a torrent of tombstones—the treeless graveyard for two millennia of Jewry.

On the lower slopes of the Mount of Olives, the Garden of Gethsemane spreads beneath the melancholy darkness of cypress trees. In early Christian times the whole hillside was covered in monasteries and oratories, but when the Persians sacked Jerusalem in 614 these holy places and their hermits were destroyed, and have left only pastel mosaics among the rocks.

The agony of Jesus in the garden was reverenced in Gethsemane as early as 333, and later in the century a handsome church was built to enshrine the traditional rock on which he had prayed to be delivered from his suffering. The Spanish nun, Egeria, who came on pilgrimage at this time, wrote how on Good Friday night huge crowds, singing hymns and faint with fasting, descended the Mount of Olives to the garden, and that when the notice of Jesus's arrest was read aloud their groans and weeping might be heard in the city above. This church was wrecked with the others by the Persians in 614, and the Crusader one that succeeded it fared little better. But early in the 20th Century the Franciscans built a long-bodied basilica— the Church of All Nations—over the Rock of the Agony.

Christ in his moment of agony in the Garden of Gethsemane is the subject of this mosaic on the façade of the Church of All Nations in the Garden of Gethsemane itself. Successive churches have stood on the site since the 4th Century. This one, built in the 20th Century with donations from 12 nations, houses the stone on which Jesus is believed to have prayed before he was arrested.

I wandered into its tiny garden, the heart of Gethsemane. Here, surrounded by scent of lavender and by drifting butterflies, eight olive trees of undiscoverable age leaned and tumbled upon the earth. Almost too old to rot or die, their wood was like stone, of a dark, incorruptible beauty. Yet leaves sprouted from them, and their branches thickened with olives.

The name Gethsemane, *Gat Shemanin*, means in Hebrew "oil-press" and among such olive trees Christ and his disciples were in the habit of sleeping on warm nights. From here in darkness the city must have lain tranquil behind its walls. Only the watch-fire of the Phasael tower would have sparked far away, while the armoured sentries on the Antonia Fortress shifted in the moonlight, and high above, the white limestone Temple hung like a phosphorous mountain-top.

I turned to go into the Church of All Nations, but found its entrance blocked by tourists, grumbling and sweating and slung with cameras. Some of the women were trying to tie scarves around their knees. I asked what was happening. "It's him," said a hefty American. "He's medieval."

In the church door a tiny old Franciscan, with the face of an El Greco saint, was turning away anybody "indecently dressed". He was saying quietly: "This is a sanctuary, not a shop."

He let me in, but closed the door on the bare knees and outraged faces. "People should prepare themselves." His faint smile did not dispel the image of a skull, so fine was his flesh over the bone. He had come, he said, from Sicily, the son of a peasant.

"You have been anywhere else?"

"No," he answered, "Sicily, Jerusalem. I don't want to go anywhere else."

"You asked to come here?"

He nodded with gleaming eyes. "I hope to die here."

Among Catholics, only the Franciscans were allowed to remain in the Holy Land after the Crusades, because the Muslims knew them to be peaceful. One by one they acquired many holy sites, and they have kept them in their care to this day.

"I think that the Lord prayed under our olive trees," he said, opening a crack in the door—the tourists had gone. "We had botanists here and they said the trees could be 2,000 years old."

The olive tree, wrote Pliny, never dies. But in A.D. 70 when Titus attacked Jerusalem he cut down all the timber around the city for siege-works, and there is no record of these trees before the 15th Century.

"But after they're cut down, saplings spring from their roots again. Olives perpetuate themselves." The monk smiled at them, as at a person. "They are all but eternal. We bottle some of their oil for pilgrims, and the rest is burnt in the lamps around the Rock of the Agony. The olive stones are made into rosaries." He held up his own; its dark stones poured through his fingers. "Feel how hard they are. The ones from Gethsemane are always small and hard. How moving they are!"

I went softly into the church. Its twilight spaces, whose columns rose to ceilings pricked with gold, suggested the closeness of a grove at night, the lift of trees and the burning of numberless stars. Through the alabaster windows, almost no light came. For a while I could see nothing but the swell of pink rock within a screen of iron thorns. Here, where the apse of the church now stands, tradition placed the agony of one who was human in his suffering, yet God enough to find no comfort in his fellow men. Alone in the presence of this rock, one can feel the hour of blood sweated in tears. One forgets to wonder who could have heard the solitary prayer to record it, and instead, in the deep of this consecrated grove of a church, imagines the staves and lanterns of the multitude come to seize Jesus. "And he that betrayed him had given them a token, saying, Whomsoever I shall kiss, that same is he; take him, and lead him away safely. And as soon as he was come, he goeth straightway to him, and saith, Master, master; and kissed him."

From this basilica it is not far up the slope to the Russian Church of St. Mary Magdalene, on the edge of Gethsemane. Its onion domes lend it a Muscovite glamour, but beneath them the pines are laden with dust and age, and the scented paths are trod by few but Arab novices. The White Russian nuns who once peopled the place are mostly dead or aged, but the spectre of Holy Czardom—heady, mystical, irrecoverably gone—pervades the place like incense after them.

A magnet to the Christians of eastern, as well as western, Europe over the centuries, Jerusalem attracted large numbers of Russians before the Revolution, and a few survive there now. This church was founded by Czar Alexander III in 1885, and the body of the Grand Duchess Elizabeth, sister of the last Czarina and a grand-daughter of Queen Victoria, is buried in its crypt. There is still living in the compound an old general who led the Imperial Cossack Guard of Czar Nicholas into Yugoslavia after their cause was lost. And the Mother Superior, a frail figure now, dressed from head to foot in white, remembered Holy Russia as a time of lost theocratic splendour, when divinity still ruled on earth. Photographs of emperors and patriarchs filled her sitting-room with their long-dead stares, and the names of Russian aristocrats fell from her lips with a sound of distant flutes. "Alexander of Serbia . . . Andrew of Greece . . . Prince Trubetzkoi . . ."

Such people—persecuted individuals and sects—are often drawn to Jerusalem; sometimes, indeed, they seem to constitute its essence. Daughter of the greatest banker in Moscow, the Mother had been in the Kremlin in 1905 when the Bolshevik insurgents killed the Czar's uncle.

"I was already 16, and I remember the service in the chapel that evening." Her face, with its thin lips and faintly hooded eyes, seemed fragile as paper. "The Czar's uncle, the Grand Duke Serge, was lying in his coffin with his head wrapped in tulle. He had no left arm at all and his right was placed over his heart, its fingers folded in the sign of the cross. The Grand

In her parlour in the Russian convent at Gethsemane, the Mother Superior remembers the Russia of the Czars, commemorated in pictures on the walls. Looking down from among them is a large photograph of the Grand Duchess Elizabeth Feodrovna, who carried out the building of the convent's church before the Russian Revolution and is buried there today.

Duchess Elizabeth was kneeling beside him in black. And their sons . . ." She lifted her hands in despair. "But now all killed, killed. . . ."

She was talking as if to herself, or to ghosts. I sat uncomfortably, eavesdropping on a past not only tragic, but sacred.

"The Grand Duchess was beautiful, a saint." The Mother Superior's voice was animated, but her dark-rimmed eyes remote. "By the will of God she is buried here. She was brutally killed with the rest of them. They were thrown alive down a mineshaft, then dynamited. One can hardly speak of such things. But her body was recovered by the White Army and taken across Siberia to Peking by a Russian monk. It was nothing short of a miracle. After so many tragedies and deaths she came to rest here, as she had wished." The Mother lifted the small silver cross around her neck. "This was found on her corpse when she was buried. It is passed on from each of our Mothers Superior to the next."

The Russia of her youth, she said, had been filled with spiritual portents. "I met saints and hermits who could see into the future clear as the old prophets. . . . In those days Russia was a land of God. Our monarchy was founded not on politics but on religion, which is the only truth. Our kings were from God and to Him they gave their oath. As a girl I saw wonderful things. And now . . ." she shook her head with sighs ". . . so many martyrs."

I looked again around the icons and photographs along her walls. Their gaze filled the room. "The world has forgotten God," she said. "My old *staretz* always said that Russia would take the first blow. And the Bible itself promised that Satan would be divided—you see it today—Russia and China!"

"Who was this *staretz*?"

"He was my spiritual father." She spread her hands in her lap. "He always saw clearly. When Rasputin wanted to see me—he often asked to see young girls of the aristocracy—my *staretz* said No. And when I heard from friends of mine, other young girls, what had happened to them"—she crossed herself swiftly—"I thank my God that I didn't go." She crossed herself again. "I can't even tell you of it."

I stood up to leave. For this one hour, caught by the emotion in the face of the Mother, I had succumbed to the rarefied world of that Russia whose pilgrims to Jerusalem had been the poorest and most fervent—and so numerous that a whole cathedral compound, now turned into offices, was built for them on an Ottoman parade-ground.

The Mother dipped her hand into a bag and pulled out papers on the Soviet treatment of Christians. "Take these. See how our martyrdom continues. But remember, the things of the world are beginning to move to their climax. Soon the merely physical will barely exist any longer. Everything is a symbol of the spirit." She dived into the bag again. "Here is a cross for you. It is made of our own olive wood from Gethsemane. And here is a reproduction of the miraculous icon of Our Blessed Virgin." She opened the door on a rush of sunlight. "And now God bless you!"

Outside the convent, on a track between blazing walls, Arab workmen were beating their donkeys into life with hoarse shouts. I sat and ate a picnic in the shade of pines. Beneath me all the slopes of the valley were banked with graves, for Jewish, Christian and Muslim sages alike promised God's blessing on Judgement Day for those buried here. The Jewish tombs covered half the Mount in their desecrated thousands. Some of their headstones had been tilted askew or broken, others reconstructed. But most lay half submerged, breathing their faint inscriptions out of dust.

I lolled like a Bacchus in the shade, eating the sweet local grapes. Some small girls came to stare at me, then sauntered away. Faint from the silted valley rose the sound of chanting, where Armenians were celebrating the Assumption of the Virgin in her traditional tomb. This rock-cut grave has been venerated since the 5th Century, and was restored by Godfrey de Bouillon, first Crusader lord of Jerusalem, who enshrined it in the handsome Abbey of Our Lady of Jehosephat.

I went down the hillside and found its entrance standing harmoniously in marble columns. Beyond them I looked down into an incense-filled

Modern gravestones—topped by rocks left by Jews as a record of their visits—crowd among ancient tombs in the Jewish cemetery on the slope of the Mount of Olives. For the devout there can be no more holy burial ground than this, lying as it does so close to the site of the ancient Temples.

darkness. Harsh chanting sounded. I began to descend. Around my feet a majestic river of steps flowed into the earth, covered in candles like clusters of glow-worms. The deep vaults and windows of the Crusaders gave way, as I continued, to the spatial calm of a Byzantine interior. I reached the sunken church. In front of the tomb—a tiny chamber ringed with the feet of vanished columns—the Armenian choir squatted on the ground in white and red robes, and rattled their golden fans. The bishop bent at the altar and prayed almost vehemently; his face was sleek under its conical cap, like a bird of prey.

I turned to ascend the steps. Through the door above, a misty daylight had changed them to long, broken threads of light. Half way up were chapels where Armenian women were lighting lamps. These, they told me, were the graves of St. Joseph and of the Virgin's parents, although I knew them to be the tombs of Crusader aristocracy.

As the Mount of Olives ascends above the Tomb of the Virgin, the route followed by Jesus fades in history and deepens in myth. Above the ruined apse of the great Eleona basilica of Constantine, where Christ was supposed to have taught his disciples the Last Things, the building of a modern church was begun after the First World War dedicated to "Peace among Nations and Peoples". But the church, like the peace, went unfulfilled, and pine trees crowd its aisles under an open sky. Beside it an eccentric Italian princess raised a sanctuary adorned with the Lord's prayer in 44 different languages—even Gaelic, Esperanto, Kurdish, Sanskrit, Samaritan—and settled down in a reconstructed Swiss chalet to await Armageddon. And to the north the fortress-like Augusta Victoria Hospital was built by Kaiser Wilhelm in anticipation, it is said, of Germany's conquering Palestine. But it became Britain's Government House instead, and then a hospital for Palestinian refugees to whom the ceiling of the chapel, painted with a scene showing the Kaiser's apotheosis as a Byzantine emperor, must be profoundly puzzling.

It was early afternoon now, and the whole sky burning. Nothing moved on the Mount but a pair of tourist camels lurching home. I wandered into the compound of Dominus Flevit, "the Lord Wept", where a modern church, shaped as a tear, commemorates the lament of Jesus over Jerusalem: "If thou hadst known, even thou, at least in this thy day, the things which belong unto thy peace! but now they are hid from thine eyes." A Franciscan monk sat in a sunhat on the terrace of the garden. Beneath us the whole city stretched like a medieval map: spires, domes, minarets. I ambled around ancient Jewish graves excavated near by; their ossuaries were clean and painted as if the bones had yet to be laid in them. A ginger cat, loping through clumps of *Spina Christi*, chased a white butterfly that took refuge on the Franciscan's hat. All about the church, where mosaic floors showed exquisite in the rock, some early monastery had basked in the city's radiance before the Persians brushed it away.

It was evening before I walked on to where a Roman lady, late in the 4th Century, had built a place called Imbomon, "Upon the Hill", in memory of Jesus's Ascension. Early pilgrims reported how this holy ground threw back anything laid on it, how the dust of the Lord's footprint perpetuated itself whenever they gathered it to take home, and how a tempest blew the faithful to their knees on the anniversary of the Ascension.

Sure enough, near the hill's crest a loutish boy grabbed my wrist and cried, "Come and see where Christ went up!" I scowled, but let myself be taken. He pulled me into an enclosure. At its centre stood the little octagonal shrine that the Crusaders had raised after the earlier sanctuary had fallen. They had built it open to the sky—a happy thought—and ringed it with a gallery now gone; but the Muslims, who also venerate Christ and his Ascension, have covered it with a plaster dome and set a mosque beside it.

"Come! Come!" the boy shouted, although his mouth was close to my ear. "Christ went up to heaven to see Muhammad!" He followed me around the octagon, angry with my coldness. The Crusader arches, blinded now in concrete, were delicate above blue-veined colonnettes. The boy pushed me inside the sanctuary. It was empty except for a rectangle of dimpled rock exposed in the floor. He forced a candle into my hand. "One dollar."

I gave him a coin.

"One dollar! This is the footprint of Christ!"

"That's enough!" I shouted, suddenly angry in the simple shrine, with its wrinkled footprint.

"This candle's worth a pound in Israel," the boy growled.

"Then take it back."

He whined on: "You want to buy a camel. . . ."

"No!"

". . . made of olive wood?"

"No."

"You want . . . ?" His voice was obliterated by the call to prayer discharged through a microphone from the minaret above us. Soon old men with pained but kindly faces went trooping into the mosque. They knelt in arthritic prayer or sat around its brightly-coloured courtyard with their sticks between their knees.

"La—llah illa—llah. . . ."

*There is no God but God. Muhammad is His Prophet.*

"One dollar," the boy whispered. "This is the place where Christ he went up into sky. . . ."

I left the shrine. Above me the summer sky, deep and empty, did not look as if it would tolerate a cloud or a bird, let alone an Ascension.

Beyond the straggle of shops and few hotels that crest the Mount of Olives I made my way to the last of its holy places: the Convent of the Ascension. Here on the summit the Abbess Tamara, Princess Bagration, first cousin to the last Czar of Russia, presides with love over a dying sisterhood of White Russian nuns. Formerly numbering 140 souls, they have dwindled to 50 now. The convent seems half deserted—only the graveyard beside it is full. From it you may look down 4,000 feet to where the Dead Sea shines steel-grey in its empty hills.

After Gethsemane, the route of Jesus's Passion becomes lost, and its very vagueness has spawned holy sites all over the city: prisons where Christ was held, columns to which he was tied and beaten, stones that cried out in horror or shouted Hosanna or that display the indentations of his bound arms and suffering feet. The Gospels say that Jesus was taken first to the home of Annas, father-in-law to the high priest Caiaphas—a mansion that may have stood somewhere in the upper city. The Armenians keep in their quarter a 14th-Century church called "the House of Annas" in lonely veneration; but its tradition is young. From Annas, Jesus was taken before Caiaphas, the high priest, whose ruined palace was pointed out as early as the 4th Century on the ridge of Mount Zion. In fact the palace probably stood far to the north-east overlooking the Temple, but the tradition continued and 1,000 years later the Armenians built a convent on the site, where they once treasured the "stone rolled back from the tomb of Christ", and where their patriarchs are still entombed beneath oval catafalques, grandiosely carved. Between 1948 and 1967 this convent stood on the edge of No-Man's-Land and was occupied by Israeli soldiers who exchanged fire with the Arab Legion on the Zion Gate. Walking one day in the half-ruined cloisters, I found their vivid tiles splashed with bullet holes. Shrubs had burst through the pavements, and under my feet the slabs of old graves, let into the flagstones, cast up the epitaphs of humbler souls buried here.

O ye, who happen on this tomb
Plant a rose on
My simple grave
I, the sacristan Krikor
Who sang prayers
And lit lamps
For forty years
On the tomb of Christ

The names of their countries—many come from afar—recalled the dispersal of Armenians over many centuries, and their emblems—keys, cups, staves, flowers—were simple and eloquent. A bookbinder, a hermit, a scribe, a candle-seller, they had lived in their quiet professions to prodigious ages, even to 106 years old.

I trailed along the chalky paths of Mount Zion by sites less credible even than this. Among them was the "Tomb of David", located here in medieval times from a misreading of the Bible, and close by rose the huge, bullet-splattered donjon of the Dormition Abbey, built on the site where Mary's

The icon painter works intently on a new panel.

## Icons from Gethsemane

In the convent of St. Mary Magdalene at Gethsemane there are three elderly Russian nuns who quietly busy themselves painting icons, the holy pictures that figure importantly in Orthodox worship. Their saints and madonnas are sold by the convent, mostly to White Russians around the world, and the money that these bring in helps support the church and sisterhood.

The painter shown here uses a mixture of traditional and modern materials, some of which she makes herself much as the artists of old did, and some of which she buys in local art shops. She relies on her companions in the convent for models, and on her imagination and piety for inspiration.

The icons of the Russian convent are in a naive traditional style, and although new, they are sometimes baked to give them a cracked, aged appearance.

life is supposed to have ended. And here, among so many questionable places, I found one that was modern and bitterly real—a shrine to the Jewish dead of the concentration camps, its vaults dripping with votive candle-grease. Gas pellets and soap made from Jewish bodies were piled as on an altar. "Earth conceal not the blood shed on thee," cried the inscription at its entrance—a memorial raised to one-third of the Jewish people in horror and unforgiveness.

I blundered along the flanks of the pre-1967 No-Man's-Land, over heaps of rubble. Its slopes were dazzling and hurt the eyes. I sat down at last in the shadow of myrtle trees, my mind still filled with Belsen and Treblinka. Below me a gang of boys had discovered a puppy in the rocks; one was holding it above his head like a small, resigned teddy-bear, while another sharpened a stick to kill it. I got to my feet in anger, but the parent dogs were already chasing the boys away, and I was left sweating but cold with the puppy sitting in the dust at my feet.

Later, as I was strolling near the church of St. Peter Gallicantu, "the Crowing of the Cock", the boys came to placate me, their pockets stuffed with stolen limes that they offered with an embarrassed roughness. They stood in silence as I peeled one; their black eyes made of me what they could. Until one of them—a lean, harsh boy with an adolescent moustache —stood in front of me and said, "You like dogs?"

"More than cruelty."

He flicked back his head in the Arab negative. "It was a dog." Then he pulled a catapult from his belt and handed it to me. "You want to buy this?" He fixed me with glittering, half-contemptuous eyes. "Look." Delving into his pockets he took out three or four cubes of mosaic—such pieces scatter these ruined slopes—and shot them over the dome of the church.

I had not time to be impressed. An old man, stumping wrathfully down the path, was shouting at the boys to stay. They ran. I imagined that he was the owner of the rifled lime orchard, and gathered my tell-tale peel into a mound and sat on it. The old man stopped opposite me in bemusement. He had a tender face, frosted in bristles. No doubt his orchard was easy picking. He forgot the boys and pointed his stick at the church, hoping to be helpful. "This", he said in croaky English, "is church where cockerel met Peter."

I nodded half-heartedly. I was conscious of the lime juice leaking up through my trousers. The old man was not convinced by my reaction and altered his theory to: "This church Peter ate cockerel."

"No," I said definitely.

"God knows best."

"Yes."

In reality this church was raised to commemorate the betrayal of Christ by St. Peter, who fulfilled Jesus's prophecy by disowning him three times before the morning cock had crowed. It was built above a 6th-Century

83

monastery, itself dedicated to the Tears of St. Peter, which in turn stands upon an ancient Jewish necropolis. But the Assumptionist Fathers, who excavated the place with more reverence than scholarship, believed that they had found the palace of the high priest Caiaphas. A round and jaunty father—bright red face under a black beret—escorted me to where three tiers of chapels enclosed a rock complex set with altars and endowed with tragic events. "Caiaphas stood here to condemn Jesus," he cried, leaping on to a boulder. "And down there"—he pointed precipitously—"Peter betrayed his Lord."

We plunged into a tomb that some later folk had carved for a horse- or donkey-stable, leaving its pillars bored with tethering-holes, and hollowing out its floor for troughs. But the priest was beside himself. He flung out his arms between the pillars. "And here the blessed Saviour was scourged! See the holes in the rock where they tied their victims!" He knelt by the troughs. "See the bowls for vinegar and water to revive the scourged ones!" He was ecstatic. We descended again into another tomb, which might later have served as a cistern. But the round priest, his face burning with happiness and effort, declared it the "Prison of Christ".

In truth the place of Caiaphas's judgement and of Peter's betrayal is unknown. But perhaps, as pilgrims to the holy places are often bruised into saying: it is not the validity of a site that matters, but its value as a focus of devotion. And indeed nothing can seem more natural—as the pilgrim tramps over memorials to trial and scourging—than the devotion of the caretaker monks and priests to their dubious charges, suffused as they are by the true pain, wherever it may really lie, of Jesus self-sacrificed. For Christians, Jerusalem must always be an ambivalent city—the blind tormentor of Christ, yet the instrument of his destiny.

# Tableaux from the East

**The massive stump of Phasael's Tower (left) and the domes of the Church of the Holy Sepulchre (right) dominate a lithograph by British artist David Roberts.**

Religious fervour, coupled with a weakness for the exotic, attracted 19th-Century travellers by the hundred to the Holy Land. For those unable to undertake the journey, the visual splendour of Christ's homeland was made available through the production of engravings and heavy ornamental tomes— many of them the work of artists who had never set foot on Palestinian soil. One who did go was David Roberts, already a successful topographical artist. In 1838 he set out from England for the Middle East, and he brought back enough original drawings to win him lasting fame for his six huge volumes entitled *Holy Land, Egypt and Nubia*. Roberts's drawings of Jerusalem gave the decayed Ottoman city a lyrical quality, while ignoring much of the squalor and poverty that shocked so many of his contemporary travellers.

The Pool of Bethesda, where Jesus healed the
lame man, was once part of the system of
reservoirs and cisterns that supplied Jerusalem
with water. Roberts drew the pool before the
area had been excavated.

Overlooking the Gehenna valley, the Tower
of David rises up from what was once Herod's
Citadel. Erroneously named after King David,
this minaret was erected by 17th-Century
Turks on top of ruined Crusader structures.

The crenellated Damascus Gate, the ultimate
achievement of Suleiman the Magnificent's
building activities in Jerusalem, stands 45 feet
high. Recent archaeological excavations
beneath it have revealed an arch probably built
by Herod Agrippa in the 1st Century A.D.

*Jerusalem. April 5th 1839.*

**The Old City, sketched from the Mount of Olives, glows with holiness in Roberts's view. He elected to omit the graves that—then and now—dot the slopes.**

# 5

# The Heart of Christendom

The heart of Christendom is the Passion of Christ: a place of execution and an empty tomb. I have reached them by a course more legendary than factual—and even here, where his mortal footsteps end, nothing is certain. The excavations around these sites, the buildings that grew above and the religious sects that dispute them could be the subject of a library, rather than a chapter. In no other city are archaeology, religion and politics so mingled. Every excavation not only realigns a controversial wall or relegates the life's work of some rival to the thin air of museum scholarship, but solidifies the claim of Israeli or Arab to the land, and slants a new light on the scriptures of Jew and Christian. The controversies are sometimes put to sleep, but never die. And while the religious belatedly propose that Christ walked in this or that direction, the vanguard of scholars and arch-aeologists is engaged in minute puzzling over an eternal mystery.

Before visiting the site of the Crucifixion and entombment, now marked by the Church of the Holy Sepulchre, I followed the traditional route of Christ to Calvary. This begins at the Convent of the Sisters of Zion, near the ruins of the Antonia—the fortress raised by Herod on a scarp above the temple. Where the stones grow from the rock like a part of itself, you may still sense the castle's power, stoop into the musty guardhouse that super-vised its gateway, or tread the terrible ramp, polished by the tramp of cohorts and cut in ridges to prevent horses from slipping.

But the convent's treasure is its pavement. Once open to the sky, now faintly lit under low vaults, it is claimed by the Sisters as the Judgement Hall mentioned by St. John's Gospel. "On this pavement," said one of them to me in a voice of hushed sorrow, "Christ was condemned to death." But she was walking over a veritable battleground of scholars—for the so-called Judgement Hall may, or may not, be the place where Pontius Pilate "brought Jesus forth, and sat down in the judgement seat in a place that is called the Pavement".

The Bible records that the Jews, refusing to be defiled by entering the house of a gentile before Passover, crowded outside the Judgement Hall and accused Jesus from there. And when Pilate, in the face of their mount-ing anger, "saw that he could prevail nothing, but that rather a tumult was made, he took water, and washed his hands before the multitude, saying, I am innocent of the blood of this just person: see ye to it. Then answered all the people, and said, His blood be on us, and on our children."

Yet this picture of Roman vacillation, say scholars, is modified by all that is known of Pilate from other sources. Experienced, brutal and indifferent

**Keeping watch over the site of Christ's tomb in the Church of the Holy Sepulchre is an icon of the Virgin Mary. Her face and hand have been blackened and effaced by age, the heat and soot of candles, and the kisses of pilgrims.**

to the feelings of those he ruled, he came of a people who were lords of the world, and whose legal code was one of their chief prides. Jesus died by crucifixion, a punishment of Roman law that the Jews shunned; and the blood of it, in the light of scholarship, thus clings to the washed hands of Pilate, not to those of the Jews. No doubt Jesus had outraged the Jewish priestly hierarchy, puppets of Rome; but he was condemned, it seems, not as a heretic but as a political Messiah, a rebel against the State, and was crucified between two *lestai*—Jewish resistance-fighters.

Some of the stone slabs of the great Judgement Court have been split by walls that fell during the siege of Titus four decades after the Crucifixion. Others the years have polished to a marble sheen, and lie underfoot faintly veined and transluscent. Still others are carved here and there with a faint web of lines. I could make out a scorpion, a star, a sword, even a miniature hopscotch square. Such *lusoriae tabulae* can be noticed in many ruins of the Roman Empire, and were simple board games, played with dice or knucklebones by soldiers far from home. You may still see Arab children in the streets playing to the same rules, trying to roll stones into little grooves.

But one of these games—the Basilinda—preserves a more sinister memory, that of the mocking of Christ. On the pavement the game appears simply as a spiked crown with the letter B. But it developed from the ghoulish Roman Saturnalia—a week-long festival popular with the legions, during which a mock king was allowed to vent his will until symbolically put to death. Precisely such a parody was made of Jesus, crowned with thorns and robed in purple; the death, however, was real.

Yet the authenticity of the great Judgement Hall is doubtful; it seems that it may simply be a part of Hadrian's forum and its guardrooms merely shops. A thesis from the Dominican school has re-established Pilate's court in Herod's old palace in the upper city, and I was glad to leave it for the giant cisterns beneath. Here, too deep to be touched by ruin, where only the drip of water defines the silence, the vaults lift from naked rock in an unearthly perfection. Every one of their stones is in place, and even in summer a faint pool gleams. Such waters could have served a garrison for ever, but now, lying chasm-like under the commotion of the city above, they echo only to their own drops which seem to be measuring the minutes, deep in this indestructible place, until the world's end.

From the convent of the Sisters of Zion the Via Dolorosa follows the traditional path of Christ to Calvary. This ancient and beautiful Way of Sorrows, which the pilgrim centuries have studded with legend, has eaten into the soul of Christendom as a symbol of suffering.

From the 14th Century, pilgrims followed a devotional route between Gethsemane and Calvary, but precisely where it led is unknown. In Crusader times another replaced it, leading from the Antonia Fortress to the Holy Sepulchre, and so began the Via Dolorosa of today. Long after-

Led by Franciscans, the procession of pilgrims that sets out every Friday to retrace Christ's steps to Calvary halts for prayers (aided by microphone) at the Seventh Station of the Cross. The course of the Via Dolorosa, marked by street signs like this one in Hebrew, Arabic and Latin, is defined by centuries of tradition.

wards, pilgrims back in their homelands laid out copies of the route and elaborated it with the 14 Stations of the Cross, until these, quaintly, became grafted on to the Way itself. Every Friday, as monks and pilgrims, often bearing a heavy cross, climb the Dolorosa, they pause at sanctuaries that cluster the Way in thick succession: the shrine of the Flagellation and the Crowning with Thorns, the Chapel of the Condemnation and Imposition of the Cross. Sometimes the pilgrims kneel in the road's dust. Sometimes they sing. Then the path flows downhill, dipping into the ancient Tyropoeon valley, before it turns and ascends. Here Jesus fell, there the Virgin fainted, here came Simon of Cyrene to shoulder the cross with him. The Way grows steep. High above its narrowness the buttresses are splashed with shrubs, and latticed windows overhang. The street climbs on tiers of steps, 16 feet above the Roman street level, where three men can hardly walk abreast and little vaulted shops hang out their wares on the walls. The pilgrims lift the cross between them, sweating and silent now, and passers-by accept them with scarcely a look. In a few minutes the procession vanishes under a low arch into the courtyard of the holiest shrine in Christendom: the Church of the Holy Sepulchre.

What should a Christian expect to find on the site of his God's resurrection? Some want a simple, personal place where nothing intrudes between miracle and man; others something numinous and awe-inspiring—a Chartres or a Santa Sophia. And almost everyone demands a reflection of his own values, both religious and aesthetic.

Almost all, of course, are disappointed. For it is not their own vision that they discover in the Church of the Holy Sepulchre. Rather it is a history of human frailty. For the place is maintained by six rival sects—Greek Orthodox, Franciscans, Armenians, Syrians, Copts and Abyssinians. Every stone and altar has been battled over, sequestrated and jealously guarded.

The church itself is less a church than a hillock of sanctuaries and chapels heaped on one another in a longing to partake of the magic at their centre. So sunk in streets, so barnacled by convents and churches and shops is this shrine, that only in the courtyard before its entranceway does its rich Crusader beauty glow. The façade rises over its courtyard with a calm, measured strength, and the carving of windows and capitals awakens its surfaces into opulent life. On one side a truncated belfry stands like the keep of a fortress. On the other, the arches are carved with birds whose heads are lost in foliage; and long-haired monkeys hold hands on a cornice.

As you enter this strangest and most significant of Christian sanctuaries, one thought obsesses the mind: Can it be genuine? Is it possible that the great church enshrines the place of Calvary and of the empty sepulchre?

Between the year of Jesus's crucifixion, perhaps in the April of A.D. 30, and the discovery of the tomb three centuries later, Jerusalem had spread beyond her earlier walls, overlapping the place of the sepulchre as it does today. It is possible, but unsure, that despite the destruction brought by the Romans, a Christian community remained almost continuously in the city and inherited a memory of where the tomb had lain. In 338, when the Roman Empire was becoming Christian, the bishop of Jerusalem received the emperor Constantine's permission to search for the holy sites. Eusebius, in his fawning *Life of Constantine*, writes that the bishop demolished a temple to Venus in the city's forum, and that "beneath the covering of earth appeared, immediately, and contrary to all expectation, the venerable and hallowed monument of our Saviour's resurrection".

Archaeology has lent support to the belief that today's church stands in the vicinity of Calvary and the Tomb. Excavations have revealed that it lies outside a city gate of Christ's time, where public executions would have taken place. But beyond this, little else is certain, and the enigmatic shrine that now rises here will continue to haunt with its unanswerable question.

Constantine separated Calvary and the sepulchre from the rock around them and spread a deep basilica in front. "I have no greater care than splendidly to adorn this holy place," he wrote, "that not only the church may be more beautiful than all the others but that even its details may excel those of any city in the empire."

Early historians claimed that Constantine's mother, the empress Helena, discovered in a near-by cistern the three crosses and the holy nails. The cross of Jesus, they said, was recognized by its power to raise the dead. It was broken up; part of it remained in Jerusalem and parts were scattered about the empire's churches, while the nails were forged into the bridle of Constantine's war-horse, and set on his helmet. Long afterwards these fragments of wood and iron multiplied all over the Christian world and were credited with calming storms and routing armies.

Constantine's basilica has vanished except for a few crushed substructures, and no comparable monument has succeeded it. So huge was

Viewed from the front, the Church of the Holy Sepulchre with its domes and roofs appears more a collection of buildings than a single structure.

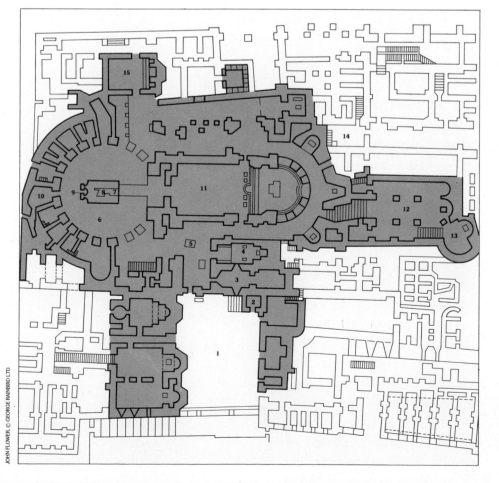

# Christianity's Shrine

The Church of the Holy Sepulchre—built over the traditionally accepted sites of Jesus's crucifixion and entombment—is a warren of chapels, holy places and historic buildings as the floor plan at left demonstrates. Calvary (3) lies near the main entrance and the Tomb stands at the centre of the domed rotunda (6). No fewer than six sects lay claim to parts of the church. Clustered around it are subsidiary chapels and monasteries.

1  Parvis (forecourt)
2  Franciscan Chapel of Our Lady of Sorrows
3  Calvary
4  Eastern Orthodox Chapel of Adam
5  Armenian Stone of Anointing, where the crucified Christ was anointed
6  Rotunda, owned by Eastern Orthodox, Armenians and Franciscans
7  Chapel of the Angel, jointly owned by Armenians and Eastern Orthodox
8  The Tomb
9  Coptic Oratory
10  Syrian Chapel
11  Choir
12  Armenian Chapel of St. Helen
13  Franciscan Chapel of the Invention of the Cross
14  Coptic monastery
15  Franciscan monastery of St. Mary

his work that the foundations of its entranceway lie far to the east of the present church, in the bowels of a confectioner's shop. For the Persians ruined it in 614, and its modestly-restored successor was thrown down again by the lunatic caliph Hakim of Egypt in the 11th Century, when the sepulchre itself was all but smashed away.

It was out of this stricken mass that the Crusaders, some 50 years after their triumph in 1099, raised up a church to shelter under one roof the multiple shrines and altars of the past. Hoisted on the gnarled shoulders of its predecessors, it still shows the beauty of the late Romanesque, but earthquake, tasteless alterations, and the screens and barriers of the rival sects have deprived it of its old harmony. In 1808 the Greek Orthodox, in a fury of restoration, not only built the trite baroque apse of today, but were so anxious to remove traces of the Catholic church that the cenotaphs of Godfrey de Bouillon and Baldwin I, the great Crusader rulers of Jerusalem, also vanished.

Now, entering where Crusader columns cluster on either side of the porch, I walked in an uproar of Franciscan chant, Armenian bells and the clashing chisels of Muslim workmen repairing the stonework. An Orthodox priest and an Israeli policeman were seated together in the entrance, with a mild old Muslim to whose ancestors the Ottomans had entrusted the keys to the church doors. But the keyhole is so high up that he has to reach it by a stepladder—and the keys to the room where the ladder is stored are kept in turn by the Greek Orthodox.

The centre of the church is a Crusader nave, but lesser shrines are dug beneath it, and even perch on its roof. Never was there such a medley of faith and stones. On every side the vaulted passageways beetle and climb, crossed by gangways and overhung by chapels. Walls are overlaid by icons, lamps, fire extinguishers. Banners drip dust. In musty side-chapels triptychs and neo-Renaissance canvases glimmer with grimy eyes, hands, swords— an endless portrayal of suffering and glory. And now and again, where in some sunken holy place a special veneration must be paid, the bare rock itself is left exposed under a downpour of silver lamps, its surface worn smooth over the centuries by adoring hands.

For this is the spiritual palace of the Eastern Church—of the Greek Orthodox above all, who inherited it from the time of Byzantium. Its duty is to the glory of God: its power is akin to magic. Little wonder that the pilgrim from northern Europe feels distress in these places, for their truth is not his. "It's disgusting," complained a female English voice passing by. "I feel sick. I feel physically sick. It's not a church, it's a rabbit warren. If Our Lord was here . . ."

Inside the entrance a tiny chapel, lifted on hewn rock, marks the site of Calvary, while to the east in the great colonnaded rotunda, stands the ugly little monument that covers the Tomb of Christ. All around these focal

Uniformed boys from the Armenian school line up at the entrance to the Holy Sepulchre, where they have come to worship. The painting above them shows the washing of Jesus's body after it was taken down from the cross—an event that, according to belief, took place on this spot.

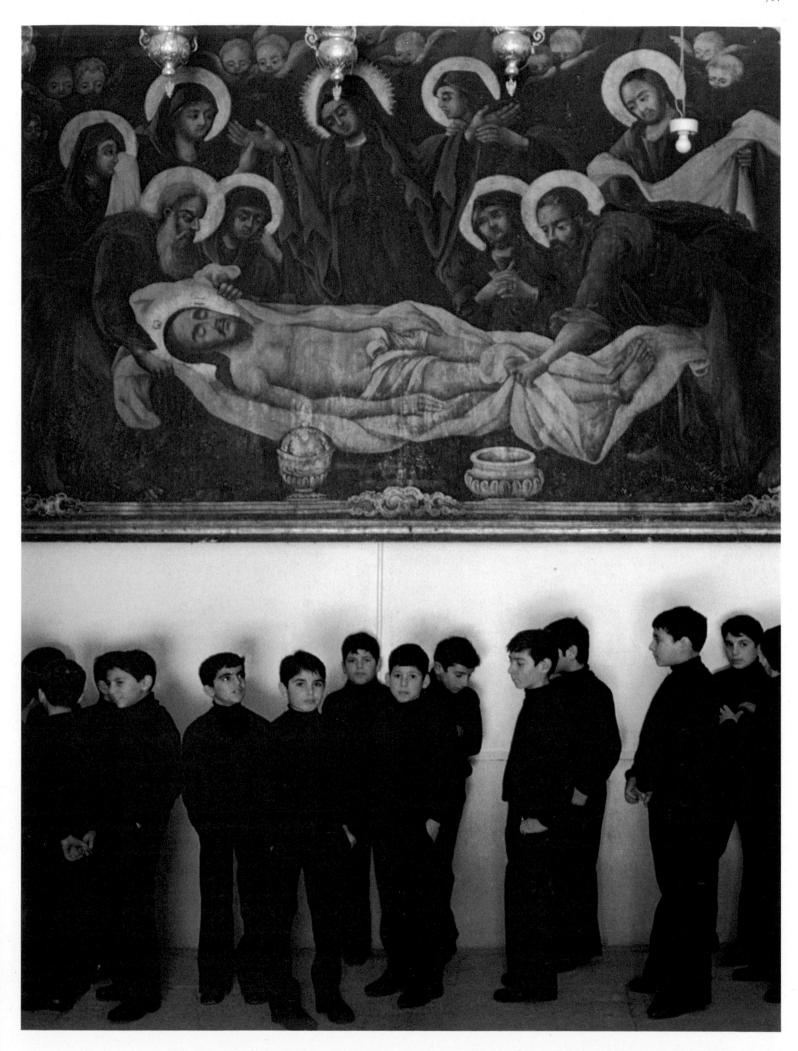

points, the cauldron of faiths is matched by the chaos of architecture: a museum of Byzantine and medieval styles, of columns and capitals that are jumbled together and sometimes upside down where restorers blundered; pillars of the time of Charlemagne, leering with stone demons; Syrian doorways; Armenian mosaics—all growing on the giant and hoary stones of Constantine's basilica.

But for the first time in centuries this will change. In the care of modern architects the Crusader church is ripening again out of its gloom. Like a patient pale from years of darkness, the newly restored choir rises strong to its vaults, and the screens and barriers of the rival sects are vanishing.

This, perhaps, was a little as medieval pilgrims knew it; and certainly they deserved better than modern tourists. Most came in the holds of merchantmen, braving Arab corsairs or the risk of Italian seamen capturing them and selling them as slaves in Muslim ports. They were the god-sent dupes of everybody. Even if they arrived safely at Jaffa, the road to Jerusalem still climbed before them, on which travellers were killed by brigands or died of thirst. The English pilgrim Saewulf, who came early in the 12th Century, wrote that on these rocky hills the earth was too thin to dig graves, and that "numbers of human bodies lie scattered in the way, and by the way-side, torn to pieces by wild beasts".

But when they reached their holiest of holies, the pilgrims were suffused only by piety and thanks. They accepted, unquestioning, the truth and magic of the place. Joyful with absolutions, they gathered its dust into phials, stole chippings from the rock of Calvary and stood wondering by the Navel of the World, an omphaloid stone that was said to have been measured by Christ's own hand. They noticed with awe how the mound of Golgotha had been rent by the earthquake at the Crucifixion, and peered into the cleft, as you may still do, to see where Adam, buried beneath the gibbet of Christ, was raised to absolution by the blood that spilt on him.

Under Turkish harassment pilgrims were sometimes locked into the church for days and slept happily among its dirt and fleas. Many were the legends that grew up during these haunted nights. In the underground Chapel of St. Helen was kept the marble bowl where Pilate washed his hands, and sometimes you might hear a gentle splashing of invisible water. Beneath the rotunda of the Sepulchre itself echoed the ghostly hammering of the blacksmith forging the nails of the Cross.

Descending towards the Chapel of St. Helen, I noticed that early travellers had incised hundreds of tiny, identical crosses in the walls. Far from the self-applauding *graffiti* of earlier or later times, each was the anonymous record of a pilgrim's passage, carved with care and humility in a world where man stood small before his God. In the chapel a finger of sunlight pierced the dome. A troupe of cowled Armenian priests was chanting. Deeper still I came into the cistern-shrine where the crosses and nails were discovered—bare except for a stone altar.

In the Church of the Holy Sepulchre the stone walls flanking the steps leading down to the underground Chapel of St. Helen are pocked with little crosses. They were carved by medieval pilgrims who had come to see the spot where the saint is supposed to have found the cross on which Christ was crucified.

A moment later the Armenians, with a belligerent burst of singing, climbed into the ambulatory and from there marched up to Calvary. The Franciscans around the Tomb, whose chant had been momentarily drowned, answered back with a choir and an organ before leaving. These minor holy wars have been going on since Crusader times, when the Knights Hospitaller tolled their bells to drown out the Latin Patriarch's prayers, and shot arrows against the church doors. The Greek Orthodox and the Franciscans went on to skirmish over the ownership of every inch of the building, and the other groups—Armenians, Syrian Orthodox, Abyssinian monks and Copts—have all fought and bribed for new rights.

So unruly did the sects become that in 1757 the Turks imposed their terrible *status quo* on the decaying church, by which nothing within it—not so much as a lamp or a picture—could be moved. For years Muslim policemen had to keep the ministers of Christ from shedding one another's blood around Calvary. And all the time the balance of Great Powers—first the Pope and Venice, later France for the Catholics, Russia for the Orthodox—was reflected here in sordid microcosm. "In disputing which party should go into it to celebrate their Mass," wrote a pilgrim in the 17th Century, "they have sometimes proceeded to blows and wounds even at the very door of the sepulchre, mingling their blood with their sacrifices."

In 1927, after earthquakes had shaken the building, the British Mandatory Power offered to restore it. But the sects could not agree even on preliminary committees, and for 40 years the crippled church stood braced in iron girders, while its paintings flaked away and its vaults cracked. Its peace is as perilous as its structure: the whole monument is threaded by invisible frontiers, along which the priests walk delicately. Only a Franciscan cat strolls from chapel to chapel in a wary ecumenical spirit.

The weaker sects, of course, have suffered most. In Turkish times the Abyssinians were edged out of their chapels on to the roof, where they built tiny cells. Whitewashed and clean, these dwellings have multiplied to a little village clustered around the dome of St. Helen and shaded by pepper trees sprouting from the stones. Sleek, kingly men with wiry beards, they live all summer in the cruel eye of the sun. They stand or sit for hours in statuesque poses, monks and nuns together, as if waiting for death.

The Copts sometimes hurl stones at them from their rooftop monastery near by, and in 1967 broke up their Easter Eve ritual. Such ceremonies have often continued at risk. In 1834, during the venerable Easter rite at the sepulchre, more than a hundred people were trampled to death as they struggled to reach the Holy Fire issuing from the Tomb. Every year the Greek Patriarch and an Armenian priest enter the Tomb, which is closed after them. Massed shoulder to shoulder outside, the faithful wait for the lamps within to be lit by "miracle", and know that this has happened when the Patriarch and the priest thrust out the flame through a hole in the Tomb's wall. Then the cry goes up: "Christ has risen!"

In medieval years it was said that an angel flew down from heaven to spark the lamps, and even in recent centuries the fire's appearance was preceded by scenes of pagan frenzy. People raced around the Sepulchre shouting and tumbling like acrobats, then picked one another up by the heels and ran them about on their hands, exposing their genitals, to the scandal of European visitors. And towards the end of the procession, wrote a caustic traveller in 1697 "there was a pigeon came fluttering into the cupola over the sepulchre, at sight of which there was a greater shout and clamour than before. This bird, the Latins told us, was purposely let fly by the Greeks to deceive the people with an opinion that it was a visible descent of the Holy Ghost."

Never have Greek and Roman Catholic been more deeply opposed than here, in their faith's heart; and as I climbed on to Calvary, which they divide between them, I could sense the flavour of this rift. I found a tiny, open sanctuary, separated into two. The Roman Catholic aisle showed a bare altar; behind it, in crude mosaic, a Christ in agony; above him the Virgin, her face carved in grief. The whole chapel, clothed with mosaic, was filled by a sense of sadness and restrained horror. At its core lay family sorrow: the *Mater Dolorosa* and the dying Son.

But beside it the Orthodox aisle was like a shout of praise, where even on Golgotha the victim was suffused in triumph. A crucified Christ of remote, almost benignant suffering hung above the altar, as if his arms were blessing it. And a gale of glory blew about him: golden lamps and candelabra, a gilded icon given by Czar Nicholas II, giant candlesticks in the grotesque taste of Kaiser Wilhelm II. Frescoed cupids puffed and fluttered over the vaults, and the blackened faces on its reredos were lapped in repoussé silver. In one aisle a woman with an airline bag prayed aloud, the tears falling behind her spectacles; in the other a cluster of French pilgrims knelt under the altar to kiss the socket which is said to have held the Cross.

Standing here, I remembered a Russian nun, delicate and old, who had tried to explain to me the difference between the Eastern and Western Churches, while we sat under pines in the village of Bethany.

"The Roman Catholics like to reach to God through visual and practical things," she said. "But we Orthodox are more mystical. Perhaps we are less bound by time than they. Time, after all, is not a permanence. This moment in which I speak—where is it?" She opened her hands. "It's gone."

An old dog came and rubbed itself against her. Beside us a small girl lay asleep under a pomegranate tree. "Sometimes we Orthodox forget the dark side of faith. Christ, after all, did not call us servants, but friends. And the Russian word for friend is *drougoi*, which gives a sense of being reflected in somebody. A friend, you see, is another of yourself. We alone were made in God's image and given his freedom."

"A two-edged gift," I teased her.

She smiled into her lap. "Yes, freedom can mean suffering. But if you suffer you learn. That is how the great saints and martyrs found God." I was aware of her own illness—she could walk only with a stick. "God will not stop man's pain," she said. "A parent's advice will never protect a child from hurt. To know fire, the child has to burn himself. And that is how we are too: the ignorant children of God." The little girl had awakened and stood staring at us—two eyes on spider's legs. "Take this one here," the nun said. "I can tell her a hundred times not to pick those pomegranates. But in a week the tree will be bare."

The girl asked: "What are you saying?"

The nun's laughter tinkled and died. Beyond where we were sitting the Judean desert shone with a derelict light. "The sin of Adam is as appalling to the Orthodox as to the Catholics," she said. "But for us damnation is not eternal. How could God blame forever what He Himself had created? He made His butterflies and grass innocent and beautiful—so why not man?"

I could not answer. Her innocence, her certainty, were too far from me.

"But we and the Roman Catholics"—she stared up into the branches of the tree—"we grow from the same trunk." She climbed to her feet. "In the end everything depends on the heart. If the heart is purified it will understand. Basil the Great—one of our foremost teachers—said that all the universe is tied together by love and sympathy. Isn't it so? Isn't it so?"

In that moment, touched by her words, it seemed to be so. But now as I wandered around the strife-sickened Church of the Holy Sepulchre, little of the kind was apparent. A Coptic priest, his fingers outstretched for money, rained rosewater on my head from his niche in the rotunda. "Kneel, kneel," he panted.

A moment later I reached the entrance to Christ's grave. Around it the chisels of Muslim workmen were clinking unseen. The dome dropped a flaking skin of paint on to everything below. I approached the ugly shrine, already hesitant. Far away the Orthodox priests were chanting on Calvary. Then I stooped through the door and into the soul of Christendom.

Smooth under my hands came a tomb-slab of orange marble, and all about it a richness of gold and flame. The guardian-priest offered me a candle, but I stood not moving. I felt as a deaf man must, to whom something is shouted. A minute later a Palestinian peasant woman entered, lifted the palms of her hands in the oldest gesture of prayer, and backed out again. I repeated to myself: This is the tomb of Christ. But the only beauty was a spray of marguerites upon the grave.

# Venerable Sects

Votive lamps suspended above Christ's tomb by various sects suggest the crowded conditions prevalent in the Church of the Holy Sepulchre.

Drawn by a possessive veneration, Christians have long cherished one site above all in Jerusalem—the Church of the Holy Sepulchre. Here the scene of Christ's crucifixion and burial has been divided into an agglomeration of chapels by six rival sects. The main participants in ownership are the Eastern Orthodox, the Armenians and—since the Crusades—the Roman Catholic Church. The Copts and Syrians are entitled to hold services there, and the Ethiopians, who were driven on to the roof in the 19th Century, preserve only traces of their former rights inside the church. Later arrivals—Russian Orthodox, Anglicans, Lutherans—built new churches close by, founded new communities or accepted the hospitality of established sects, finding their own various ways to participate in the Christian experience of Jerusalem.

Franciscans like these are custodians of many of Jerusalem's shrines.

## The Franciscans

The Franciscan Order, reputedly established in the Holy Land when St. Francis travelled there in 1219, has been the chief representative of the Roman Church in Jerusalem ever since the Crusader period. The simple Franciscan Chapel of Calvary inside the Church of the Holy Sepulchre stands on the spot where the Crucifixion is believed to have taken place.

Dimly lit, a modern mosaic of the Crucifixion rises sombrely—and symbolically—behind the altar of the Franciscan Chapel on the site of Calvary.

An Orthodox priest on duty borrows a votive candle to read his paper.

## The Eastern Orthodox

Jerusalem's predominant Christian community is the Eastern Orthodox, whose chapel in the Holy Sepulchre shares Calvary with the Franciscans. The community owes its prominence to its development from the early Byzantine Empire and partly to the preference given it over the rival Roman Church by Ottoman rulers reluctant to encourage a strong Western presence.

Only a few feet from the plain Franciscan chapel (previous page), a blaze of candlelight sheds a golden lustre on the Orthodox Chapel of Calvary.

A White Russian nun greets a visitor at the main gate of her convent.

## The Russian Orthodox

Since their presence in Jerusalem dates only from the 18th and 19th Centuries, the Russian Orthodox have no traditional rights in the Holy Sepulchre: they participate there in the services of their fellow Orthodox, the Greeks. But under Czarist patronage they acquired a hallowed site (above) and established two communities of nuns on the Mount of Olives.

**A commemorative fresco and a fall of steps flank an archway through which Jesus is supposed to have passed as he carried the Cross to Calvary.**

Unmistakable in their pointed hoods, Armenian monks pass by a grille.

# The Armenians

The cohesive national community living in the Old City's ancient
Armenian quarter, with its great church, rich convent and
religious seminary, shows the strength of their religious heritage.
Armenian Christians have been in Jerusalem for over 1,500
years. Like the Eastern Orthodox and Roman Catholics, they
have secure rights in the Church of the Holy Sepulchre.

Choir, congregation and hooded clergy celebrate the liturgy in the huge church of St. James, rich with lamps, wall-tiles and fine carpets.

Shrouded against the wind, an Ethiopian monk rests by his rooftop cell.

## The Ethiopians

In the vicissitudes of its history the small but ancient Ethiopian, or Abyssinian, sect has lost most of the rights of possession it once had in the Church of the Holy Sepulchre. The monks now live a humble, contemplative life on the roof of the chapel of St. Helen, stubbornly guarding their privileges against the rival claims of the neighbouring Copts.

On the roof of the Holy Sepulchre, interlocking walls and arches of different periods give the Ethiopian monks a small, complex world of their own.

# 6

# The Dome of the Rock

A garishly-lit café, offering little but soft drinks, stands today where the two main streets of ancient Jerusalem crossed. The huge pillars that once ornamented this intersection still stand half sunk in dust. They prop up the café roof and have been crudely painted. Sitting here, where the Arab and Jewish quarters touch, I could watch the human traffic churning its way down the long Street of the Chain, still Roman in its straightness.

I sat in that state of torpid suspension that the Arabs call *kayf*, and listened to an incongruous yet characteristic sound of the Arab quarter: the click of billiard balls. Behind me, four young Muslims, with serious expressions, were playing as keenly as Englishmen in a country club.

This rather ordinary scene—Arabs playing a British-imported game among the columns of Imperial Rome—could symbolize the Muslims' flair for adapting foreign ways to themselves, something that they have been doing ever since they captured Jerusalem in A.D. 638. Around the billiards table even the faces were typical of this assimilation. One man looked like a Mongoloid Turk; another resembled a north Arabian; a third had a shock of red Crusader hair, while a fourth appeared Greek.

All would have called themselves Arabs, and the religion of Muhammad binds them each to each in a common culture and outlook. Yet this faith is complex and many-faceted. The traveller in Jerusalem may be amazed to learn that the Arabs reconsecrated the site of the Jewish Temple by building the Dome of the Rock there, and that the Koran is filled with devout references to Noah, Abraham, Moses and Christ.

To understand this anomaly one must look back to the 7th Century, when the core of the ancient world was split between the Emperor of Byzantium and the Persian King of Kings. It was then that an obscure message from Arabia arrived at the court of each monarch. It warned him to renounce his idolatrous religion and follow the One God, and was sent in the name of an unknown prophet, Muhammad of Mecca. The king apparently received the message with disdain; the emperor was mildly curious. Yet the message was ominous, for within 50 years the Persian dominions had vanished and the Muslims were at the walls of Constantinople.

This explosion from the Arabian peninsula was only the latest of many. During the preceding 3,000 years other Semitic peoples—Amorites, Arameans, Canaanites, Hebrews—had broken northwards in search of deeper pastures. But the Arab coming was more sudden. The pressure of over-population, together with the unifying discipline of the One God, carried them irresistibly through countries already exhausted by war.

A group of Arab women in typical Palestinian clothes—long muslin or floral dresses with ample muslin scarves—climb the steps up to the Dome of the Rock. The pillars belong to one of eight stairways leading to the shrine.

They did not arrive as religious fanatics. Instead Muhammad, who had come into contact with Jews and Christians in Arabia, saw himself as the last of the great biblical seers whom the Koran acknowledges with such reverence. Originally the Prophet had ordered his followers, when they prayed, to turn to Jerusalem, the centre of the world. Only when the Jews resisted Islam did his allegiance turn to Mecca, and even then it was the Jews' practices that he repudiated, not their religion; for "who but a madman could reject the religion of Abraham?" runs the Koran. "We have chosen him in this world and in the next he will be among the just." Christ himself was called the second among prophets; in Islamic belief he was crucified only in effigy, and his body taken by God into heaven.

Because the city was already holy to them, the Muslims' siege of Jerusalem in A.D. 638 was a gentle one. The Byzantine patriarch Sophronius, who knew of Arab clemency to other towns, went out to discuss peace with the caliph Omar on the Mount of Olives and was granted security of his people and churches. So the gates were opened and the urbane and aged patriarch entered them with the dusky little caliph in rags at his side. A Muslim tradition runs that as they approached Jerusalem it became the turn of the caliph's servant to ride his camel, so Omar alighted and entered on foot, in the simple democracy of the desert.

The city that the Muslims found was no longer at its zenith. Only 30 years before, richly endowed by its Byzantine rulers, it had flowered into commercial wealth and architectural splendour: the most precious jewel of all Christendom. But already religious controversy was staling the city's spirit, and then came the Persian sack of 614, when every church was gutted and the cream of its citizens led into exile.

Entering this sobered city, still full of ruins, the caliph Omar asked Sophronius to take him to the site of the Temple of Solomon: the holy place of his people's adopted prophets. But the patriarch delayed. He was afraid that Omar planned to rebuild it for the Jews. Besides, during the Persian sack a quarter of a century before, the Jews had helped the invaders to massacre the Christians and burn their churches; and in retaliation the Christians had covered with excrement the great Rock where the Jewish altar had stood. So Sophronius took the caliph instead to the Church of the Holy Sepulchre and other Christian shrines, and it was only by chance that Omar discovered the Temple site. Its entrance was so choked with dung that he could only squeeze into the enclosure on all fours, while the patriarch crawled in front, and with his own hands the caliph was the first to pick up the filth from the holy Rock and hurl it into the valley. Here, where Solomon—so Muslims came to believe—had ordered the demons to quarry jacinth and emerald for his Temple and to dive for its pearls in the depths of the sea, Omar built a makeshift wooden mosque.

Much of this is legend, but it hangs in a frame of truth. Omar was generous to the city, and its population, itself largely Semitic, must have

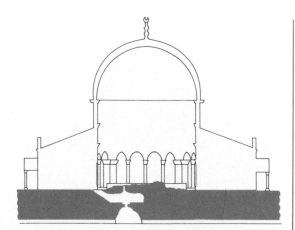

A cross-section of the Dome of the Rock shows the irregular profile of the rock itself and the two caves—once probably cisterns—that lie beneath it. A staircase leads from the shrine's interior to the upper cave, which Muslims call "the Well of Souls" because of the spirits that are supposed to pray there. A floor now seals the lower cave, "the Abyss of Chaos", linked by a channel to Jerusalem's ancient water system.

regarded the Arabs as desert cousins, proud but uncouth. The Arabs in turn were more anxious to rule than to convert. Their attitude to both Christians and Jews was lenient for its day, and the fact that Jerusalem still contains its large and healthy Orthodox and Armenian quarters is the lasting mark of their tolerance.

To the Muslims Jerusalem, although a spectre of its old self, was civilized, rich and awesome in sanctity, and their legends proliferated around it. They came to call it *El-Kuds*, "Holiness", third of the sacred cities after Mecca and Medinah; and just as medieval cartographers would portray the city as the heart of a flower, whose petals were continents, so the Muslims conceived of the earth as a fish, whose head is in the rising sun, whose tail is in its setting and the centre of whose back upholds the Holy Rock of Jerusalem. Many were the friends and warriors of Muhammad who came to be buried here, and because Jerusalem had been conquered by Omar, the Prophet's friend, it was considered to be Muslim holy land—the personal legacy of God to His servants. From an open gate in the city of paradise, said the sages, the light of God's compassion streamed down upon Jerusalem forever; its very dew fell from the heavenly gardens, and could cure all ills. Those who died here were assured of their place in heaven, and at the Day of Judgement, it was said, God would descend to Jerusalem hemmed by black clouds and a swarm of angels, while Jesus would judge the dead.

But the focus of Muslim tradition was the Rock, the bare hillcrest where the Temple's altar had stood. The Arab mind, which loves to garnish the physical with the spiritual, peopled it with 70,000 angels who stood eternal guard around it. Half the Old Testament patriarchs were frogmarched into service: upon this hoary stone Adam had risen out of dust, Noah's Ark ground to its final resting place, Abraham prepared to sacrifice Isaac, and Jacob dreamed of angels climbing their golden ladder between earth and paradise. The Kaaba meteorite enshrined in Mecca may be more holy to Muslims—for it fell out of heaven—but the Rock of Jerusalem, they say, is the foundation stone of the world, under which Solomon was shown the entrance to the Celestial City, and on the day of Resurrection it is the Kaaba stone—in a tricky point of etiquette—that will fly through the sky and pay a courtesy visit to the Rock.

Yet one belief above all established the Rock in the Muslim soul—they believed it the scene of Muhammad's night-visit to heaven. "Glory be to Him who carried His servant by night from the Sacred Mosque to the Far-away Mosque," declares the Koran, and devout minds conceived the Far-away Mosque to be the one at Jerusalem, the farthest point of pilgrimage. Muhammad flew from Mecca on his sacred steed *El-Burak*, say the *Traditions*, and from this Rock was lifted by Gabriel into the stars. There, Dante-like, he mounted through all the spheres of hell and paradise, and spoke with Adam, Jesus and the Great Ones before him.

In spite of this belief, 50 years seem to have elapsed before the Rock was covered by any proper building—and even then it was accomplished for political motives. In 680 the caliph in Damascus, Abd al-Malik, found himself faced by an anti-caliph in Mecca. This deprived him not only of prestige but of the revenue from the great Mecca pilgrimage. One of the most cunning of his dynasty, he set about deflecting the pilgrimage to Jerusalem, which lay within his own territory, and by 691, using seven years' revenue from the province of Egypt, he had erected the first and perhaps most glorious monument of Islam, the Dome of the Rock.

Looking at the sanctuary now, a man might imagine that the Arabs had brought some vision of unity out of their wilderness, and realised it here in the genius of faith. But this is not true. The Dome of the Rock, like most beautiful buildings, was the harvest of complexity and long tradition. Its architects and craftsmen were not Muslim, but the mingled and Hellenized peoples whom the Arabs found in Jerusalem, a people steeped in culture. Nor did the sanctuary find its models in Arabia, but looked rather to the Holy Sepulchre itself—exactly reproducing the diameter of the church's dome—and to the mausolea of ancient Rome.

Yet Islam, more subtly than most civilizations, moulded the arts of others to itself, and the Dome's classical proportions acquired an Islamic veneer. The Muslims, who detested images, decorated it with geometric designs and inanimate objects; and later its outside mosaics were replaced by Persian tiles of almost violent splendour.

Emerging from shaded streets, I approached the sanctuary over a paved emptiness where no wind stirred. Pine and cypress trees cast strange, rough glades of shadow on the stone. A scattering of little buildings, their purpose ended or forgotten, showed domes or arches here and there. So choked are the narrow lanes of the Old City that the sky is rarely noticed, but here it arched in a bowl of porcelain blue, deep and absolute from horizon to horizon. Around the enclosure the patched walls and rebuilt colonnades were like the bones of a mammoth, picked and picked again. For the whole court—whose proportions were dictated 2,000 years ago by Herod —is haunted by the ancient Temple: its lost order, its remembered life.

Underneath it is honeycombed with cisterns and wells. Along its perimeter rise medieval minarets. And gates with sonorous names lead from it into the city—the Gate of Darkness and the Gate of Iron; the Gate Beautiful, the Gates of Absolution and the Tribes.

"*Wullah!*" cried a voice behind me. "You want a guide?"

"No . . ." The young man, heavy and half-shaven, looked a mine of misinformation.

"This was the Temple of Solomon," he began remorselessly, "and afterwards the Temple of Herod and afterwards . . ."

Now, at the world's centre, with tiles and golden cupola renewed, the Dome of the Rock stood precise and assured. From the spread of an

The paved platform on which the Dome of the Rock stands stretches to shrines and free-standing arches. Muslim legend holds that the scales, used to weigh souls, will hang from these arches on Judgement Day.

octagonal base its beauty lifted with a sense of almost grave preordainment to a dome like the surge of a golden flower. So sudden and perfect was this sanctuary, set in its empty field, that I could imagine no other here, let alone the Temple of Herod.

Steps mounted to the platform on all sides, where free-standing arches looped in a broken screen. I climbed them slowly. The shrine filled the sky ahead. Its tiled blues and greens shone with a fierce, prismatic symmetry. I saw the faience lattices of windows and little porches on veined columns.

In the lower walls the veining in a pair of marble panels suggested swallows drinking from a bowl; these birds, say the Muslims, quarrelled with King Solomon who turned them into stone.

Around the entrance a group of aged *hajjis*—men who had made the pilgrimage to Mecca—were hobbling in snowy turbans. Old in years and older in tradition, they seemed to carry their faith sadly. One of them tentatively smiled at me, and finding me ready to listen, poured out his nostalgia. Nothing was as it had been. Religion itself seemed to be dying, he said, and man was slighting his Creator.

"Even this is no longer a place of God." He looked up at the golden dome, the bitter radiance of his past. "People no longer come here for prayer, merely for pleasure."

"You mean tourists?"

"Yes. But Muslims too." His eyes strayed to one of the guards, lithe as a monkey with his rake and broom. "Look at that man there. He is typical of our people now. If he prays he can only follow the rules—standing, kneeling, sitting like a machine. That is all. Such a man cannot speak from here"—he laid a frail fist over his heart. "Such a one cannot read and will not listen—so how will he reach God?" He bowed his head. "How can you know a person if you have not met him?"

"Perhaps he knows God within his limits," I suggested piously.

But the *hajji* pulled himself upright with an old-world dignity. "Why do we pretend? He knows nothing. Few of our people any longer know any-thing." His eyes showed large and wistful behind their spectacles. "Yet scholar's ink, we say, is holier than martyr's blood. If we do not learn, we cannot stand against other faiths."

"Or against the world."

He frowned. "We've always known the world."

This fear of other religions was, I think, new to him. More than Christianity, which grew up in persecution, Islam needs to live under its own rule, secure among its own people. With Israeli rule, this has gone. The old man's voice had turned a little querulous. "We in Islam don't reject the Jews' or Christians' prophets. Not at all. It's only they who reject ours." He took off his glasses, held them to the light. "We do not say that Islam is the only expression of the will of God. But it is the last and most perfect." Flies had settled on his face but he did not brush them away. "When I pray I feel near to something great. It may not be deeply good or bad; but its quality is greatness. How can I express it?" He glanced at the sky. "It is at the edge of eternity . . ."

He replaced his spectacles. Behind them his eyes seemed to notice again the poverty of the people around him: peasants trooping up the steps, and the simian guard leaning on his rake. "You see, the Ottomans crushed us. We had 400 years of them—and they did not even understand how to treat their friends. My own uncle went as a delegate from Jerusalem to Istanbul in the time of the sultan Abdul Hamid—who was a madman. When my uncle complained about the taxes, they tried to murder him. In those days our very bones were taxed out of us."

"It must get better." My voice, I noticed, held more sympathy than hope.

"Materially, perhaps," he said. "We'll go on living. My own family has been here 700 years. We will not die tomorrow." He paused, then said with a rueful pride. "I am descended from Khalid ibn-Walid, 'the Sword of God'—he who captured Damascus!"

I watched him walk away over the blazing stones, then under the crumbling medieval façades below, his shoulders thrust a little back, but his head staring at the ground. He seemed to carry in his person all the pride and frustration of his people.

Many of Jerusalem's Muslims—there are some 60,000 in all—live crowded to north and west of the Dome of the Rock. Upon its sacred ground, which they call *Haram as-Sharif*, "the Noble Sanctuary", no house has ever intruded, although the area is almost as large as their entire quarter in the Old City, whose dwellings are fearfully cramped. All live within call of its minarets. There is no old family among them that has not some traditional duty, now probably defunct, in the great shrine. It is at once their glory and their reproach. For looking at the Dome of the Rock, the Muslim is inevitably reminded of what he once was—master of half the known world, and the favoured of God. Subconsciously, at least, he must ask himself what went wrong. In Jerusalem, far from the oil-rich Persian Gulf, the Arabs' new wealth seems still to belong to dreams. And the Muslim heart, the old *hajji* said, was shrivelling in its body.

Inside the shrine the vivid blue and gold of the exterior was forgotten. I entered a denser richness. I found myself walking around an ambulatory, whose carpets were noiseless underfoot, beneath the subdued brilliance of painted ceilings. The beams were bound in repoussé and gilded copper, many of them exquisite, and stained glass windows hung in shadow; while all around, the ancient columns, plucked from some older building, held the dome dazzling above. I moved clockwise as the faithful do, mesmerized —for at the centre of all this reverence, more ancient than carved wood or marble, the Rock of the hill summit erupted savagely into the sanctuary.

Old women, wrapped in white veils, went shuffling before me, whispering prayers through tattooed lips. I could hear them all around the ambulatory.

El-Kas, the cup, is the principal ablution fountain in the sacred precincts of the Dome of the Rock and the Aqsa Mosque. It is surrounded by low stone benches upon which men sit to perform the obligatory washing of hands, heads and feet before praying in the mosque.

As if the Rock were a sun and they the planets in its orbit, they walked in an age-old tension of worship: drawn by longing but withheld by awe. Under the gilded cage where two of Muhammad's hairs are kept, they touched his footprint carved in rock, and finding it to be scented ran their hands with little cries over each other's faces.

In the time of Abd al-Malik, the builder of the shrine, the Rock was bathed every Monday and Thursday in saffron, ambergris, rosewater and musk. Silk curtains were drawn around it, while servants with scented hands and feet walked over it in procession, carrying gold and silver censers. High in the dome, on a golden chain, dangled the "horns of the ram that Abraham sacrificed", along with the diadem of Chosroes, the Persian King of Kings conquered by the Arabs.

The dome has changed since then. It fell during an earthquake in 1016, and in the 14th Century it was reconstructed and covered with painted and gilded plaster in low relief, the product of Indian artists. This brilliant work, like the bloom of some polychromatic flower, momentarily eclipses everything around it. But a second later the eye travels to the base of the dome, where green and gold mosaics have survived from the shrine's foundation. They are bizarrely beautiful and extravagant. Between the windows and in a deep band beneath, the artists portrayed vases with bulbous, jewelled bodies. Out of each one writhes an eerie mélange of tendrils and wings— the cloud of genii before they have formed—and about them twist vine patterns, studded with mother-of-pearl.

It is common knowledge among the Muslims that as Muhammad rose to heaven the Rock began to rise faithfully with him; but the angel Gabriel held it back, and you may see his fingermarks still. So was formed the cave beneath it, called *Bir el-Arwah*, "the Well of Souls", which lies only lightly above "the Abyss of Chaos", where the rivers of paradise spill out into eternity. The cave's floor is laid with simple straw mats, and Muslims pray here in a fervid absorption. They say that under the floor you may hear the voices of the dead sighing together with a noise like waters, and a pavement has been laid above to prevent the faithful from setting their mouths to the cracks and chatting with the departed. In earlier times all those who had prayed here and had circumambulated the Rock above, were issued with a certificate to take to their graves and show to the gatekeeper of paradise as a ticket of admission.

But as I stood in the cave a harsher memory arose. Above me a funnel had been bored upwards to the Rock's surface. This, almost certainly, was the "perforated stone" where the Jews first wept for their fallen Temple. From an altar above it the blood and water of sacrifice may have drained down into the grotto. Here, perhaps, was the very threshing-floor that David had bought and on which Solomon had built the Temple.

As I left the Dome of the Rock, a low wind was blowing along the courts. I wandered southwards in their emptiness: a flagged field peopled

A blind man, marked as a pious Muslim by his white turban, approaches a mosque. The boy may be his pupil, or perhaps just a passer-by fulfilling his duty to help those whose disability shows that God has touched them.

During his absence, the family of a pilgrim to Mecca traditionally paints the outside of his house with patterns and symbols (right). The paintings once served as charms to safeguard the traveller, but now they are simply decorations that advertise his journey.

## Outward Signs of Piety

The quiet current of religious life flows uninterrupted amid the turmoil of Jerusalem's Muslim quarter, and although much of it goes unremarked—for Islam is not a hierarchical or ostentatious faith—signs here and there confirm the devotion of Allah's followers to the duties of their religion, including prayer, almsgiving, fasting and pilgrimage. It causes no comment if at the muezzin's call someone interrupts a conversation to produce a prayer mat and kneel towards Mecca. In the Muslim community, piety arouses sincere respect, and no more so than when a householder proudly displays evidence of a pilgrimage to Mecca.

The clear symmetrical outlines of the Dome of the Rock appear in a painting (right) on a pilgrim's house-front, along with a message giving thanks on behalf of the owner and his wife for a Mecca pilgrimage.

by legend. So crowded with invisible spirits is it, wrote a pilgrim, that "should I hit you a blow upon the forehead, it would light upon the forehead of some prophet or angel". David, Solomon, Gabriel, Alexander the Great, Jesus, St. George—many are the heroes who have prayed here.

A blind man went tapping over the pavements, smiling. All over the platform stood small and enigmatic shrines, fountains and gateways harbouring strange stories. Across the free-standing arches around the Dome, it is said, will hang the scales of Judgement Day; and a little sanctuary near by, called the Dome of the Small Rock, enshrines a legendary stone that Nebuchadnezzar carried away to Babylon, and the Israelites brought back. In a tiny mosque called the Throne of Solomon, the great king propped himself upon his staff in death, so that the demons who served him believed him still alive; but after a long time, runs the tale, a worm gnawed through the stave. The king crashed to the ground, and the demons overran his kingdom. In a little prayer-niche, say the Arabs, the Virgin Mary worshipped, facing Mecca. To the Muslims, Mary is a figure of veneration who carried in her womb the Word of God. Because of this miraculous birth, they believe that while the body of Muhammad lies in his tomb at Medinah, Jesus lives on, his human body incorruptible in paradise.

"We don't reject Christ as a prophet," an Arab lawyer told me. He was a man with a pale, intelligent face. "It is the Bible and Church we reject. This splitting of God into three, this harping on grace and original sin—these are degrading to God and pretentious for men. Altogether, Christianity is too idealistic. It cannot grapple with day-to-day things as Islam can." His eyes bulged good-humouredly. "For instance, it says you must turn the other cheek if you are struck. Now that is laudable—but if Christians had all done it there would be none left. So what happens? They say one thing and do another, which is not healthy. In Arabic we have a maxim 'If you want to be obeyed, don't ask the impossible'!"

"Does God, then, not demand perfection?" I found myself frowning.

"The Koran says that you may pay back transgressors only to the degree of their hurt. But it adds that if you forgive, God will reward you. There you have both a limit to revenge and an incentive to good."

He himself, I thought, showed that dignified security in tradition that is the hallmark of a living Islam. "Like the Jews," he said, "we think of ourselves as a special people. But we do not exclude others as they do. The Koran says the Muslims were chosen not as a birthright, but because of their goodness." I wanted to ask—but this was hard—why Islam had grown arid with the centuries. But the sensitive lawyer seemed to anticipate this and murmured almost to himself: "We must have sinned against God."

The gravity of the pious Muslim, I think, grows from a lack of strain. One sees such a look in the face of old and dignified servants. God may be far away, but His commands are specific. Nor is sin a slight on a loving Christ, a fall from grace, but is a simple offence against law.

"God is beyond Jesus and Moses and Muhammad," said the lawyer, "beyond even this world. It is often said that we Muslims are crushed with fatalism. This is not so—but we never lose the sense of God's greatness. And surely this is a corrective in life? That expression of ours *Inshallah*— if God wills!—is both a check to pride and a consolation for failure."

Indeed the will of God can be formidable in Islam, and sometimes He seems to display no moral essence. "God leads astray," says the Koran often and chillingly, He is "the One Who brings damage". Fate, necessity, decay. The lawyer was not pleased by this idea, but it shows, perhaps, a profoundly honest apprehension of the universe. God, it implies, is greater than good or evil: those concepts belong to man. Such, at least, is an element in Islam, and Muslims may have paid for it in their soul.

I watched them praying in the Aqsa Mosque near by, bending and kneeling on a pool of mulberry carpets; hands behind ears, on knees; foreheads to ground. A grandfather clock—the Muslims love these clocks —dinged faintly beside them. This mosque, too, is old, but much restored. It spreads in the great court south of the Dome, and is no less steeped in sanctity; for traditionally, as its name says, it is the "Far-away Mosque" of Muhammad's miraculous journey from Mecca; and some believe that God will pardon the sins of those who worship here.

But disasters have dogged it. Already by the 10th Century a native of Jerusalem wrote of the Aqsa as a modern mosque in which the older part lay merely "like a beauty spot, in the midst of the new". And it is the same today. A forest of glacial Carrara columns, gift of Mussolini, upholds the painted ceilings sent by King Farouk. And the heart of the mosque was gutted when a mentally unbalanced youth set fire to it in 1969. The lovely dome now hangs in shreds. With it the inlaid pulpit, a Damascene master-piece of the 12th Century, was reduced to a heap of cinders.

But even here, in the sacred precincts of the Aqsa and the Dome of the Rock, not destruction, but continuity, may be remembered. For the Crusaders, when they took the city in 1099, did not damage the shrines. Instead their Templar knights, perhaps wiser than they knew, adopted the Dome as the "Temple of the Lord". They mounted it with a cross and fastened to its door a gold and diamond effigy of Jesus.

Doubtless the Muslims under Saladin, when they recaptured the city in 1187, feared for their holy Rock. But they found it had been set with an altar and shielded by a beautiful iron grille. The only damage had been caused not by anger but by love—for pilgrims from all over Christendom had reverently chipped away pieces of the Rock and carried them home.

# The Jewel Box of Islam

**Emblazoned around the exterior of the Dome of the Rock are verses from the Koran and formal patterns symbolizing the harmony of Allah's universe.**

For nearly 1,300 years the Dome of the Rock has sheltered an outcrop of stone that is sacred to Muslims and Jews alike. King Solomon built his Temple upon this rock, and traditions claim that Muhammad journeyed to heaven from it, thus making it the third holiest site in Islam, after Mecca and Medinah. The caliph of Damascus raised the shrine in 691 to draw pilgrims—with their money and political allegiance— to Jerusalem, and his craftsmen decorated its exterior with gold mosaics. In the middle of the 16th Century the Ottoman Turks replaced the decaying mosaics with 45,000 dazzling Persian tiles, repaired, in turn, during several succeeding centuries. Today, after an eight-year restoration by Arab governments, the Dome of the Rock is once again one of the finest monuments in the Muslim world.

Restored to its original lustre with modern gold-plated aluminium, the dome rests upon the perfect octagon of the shrine. Over 10,000 sheets of brass gilt—legend says that they were sheathed with pure gold—covered the first dome of 691. When it collapsed in 1016, the dome was rebuilt in sombre lead.

The entrances to the dome are oriented exactly to the compass; the south entrance— shown here—faces Mecca. "God, the Eternal" is written in the right-hand square above the porch and repeated in mirror image in the left-hand one, while Koranic verse in the shadows under the arch exhorts the faithful to pray in the direction of Mecca.

Ancient columns, taken from Roman and other
buildings, lift up the gilded dome. Seventh-
Century mosaics gleam beneath arched windows,
some containing 16th-Century stained
glass. They help make the building
a treasure house of art from different cultures.

Two rings of marble columns with gilt capitals
—seen through the open bronze doors—form
a double passageway around the interior.
The wood ceiling is decorated with gold enamel
paints, and the columns are linked by thick
beams overlaid with stone and bronze.

A kaleidoscope of arabesques, the inside of the dome is the masterpiece of 14th-Century artists imported from India, who worked in plaster. The Arabic writing in the circular bands near the rim and in the centre has been inscribed and re-inscribed by successive sultans in the traditional Muslim manner of recording benefactors and their gifts.

Under the dome lies the shrine's physical and spiritual centre—the scarred and chiselled Rock itself. The mysterious light-filled hole may have been used to drain blood from animal sacrifices in Israelite times. No one knows who cut the ridges along the top and right-hand edge, but devout Muslims believe they were made by the Archangel Gabriel as he struggled to keep the holy Rock from ascending to heaven with Muhammad. The reliquary on the Rock in front of the thick column at centre-left holds two hairs from the Prophet's beard.

# 7

# Crusaders and Muslims

Hidden behind bazaars in the Christian quarter of Old Jerusalem is the small, silver-domed Church of St. John. It stands in a court filled with lemon trees, and even the priest who escorted me was uncertain of its history.

"It belongs to all ages," he said offhandedly, then looking towards the altar added with pride: "We have a reliquary which contains the skull of the Baptist! You see how old the church must be!"

I silently dismissed this legend—there are enough heads of the Baptist in Christendom to have furnished a hydra—but the age of the church was complex. Its crypt was once a chapel, and was built by an exiled Byzantine empress as long ago as the 5th Century. Now it lay empty—our feet crunched strangely in its silence—and over it the Crusaders had raised a new church that had fallen and been replaced.

These strata of faith and decay may be traced all over the city. An Arab layer lies beneath the Crusader, the Crusader layer beneath the Mameluke and the Turkish. During the 1,200 years between the building of the Dome of the Rock and the 20th Century, Jerusalem's decline was caused less by the old, spectacular disasters, than by a gradual paralysis that crumbled mosques, houses and churches into each other. The colonnaded streets of the classical age were smudged and overlaid by the chaos and warmth of life, and the Old City acquired the appearance it preserves to this day.

After building the Dome of the Rock, the Aqsa Mosque and the palaces that attended them in the south, Jerusalem's Arabs were to produce little else of architectural significance. The capital of their empire passed from Damascus to distant Baghdad and although for a while Jerusalem prospered, its insecurity increased. Late in the 9th Century the southern walls, erected more than 400 years before to enclose a swelling Christian metropolis, were drastically shrunk to the lines that they follow today, and the slopes of Ophel and Zion, where David's city lay forgotten, were left defenceless. Mukaddasi, an Arab native of Jerusalem, wrote of the city with uncertainty. Its people, he said, were known for their piety, frankness and chastity; yet the schools and mosques were empty, the public baths the dirtiest in the world, taxes exhorbitant and "everywhere the Christians and Jews have the upper hand". Within another century, by the eve of the Crusades, earthquake, religious fanaticism and the 21-year rule of new invaders—the Seljuk Turks—had devitalized the city.

The Christians, clustered about the Holy Sepulchre where the Christian quarter spreads today, were no longer so numerous. Muslim proselytizing had reduced and isolated them. Gone were the ostentatious basilicas of

Stepping out into a quiet street of the Muslim quarter, an old Arab wears a tasselled fez. This headgear dates from the days of Ottoman Turkish rule in Jerusalem, which came to an end in 1917 when the British took over.

their zenith; and the Jews, used to better treatment under Islam than they received now, huddled in the city's north-west corner.

It was partly out of indignation in Europe over reports of Seljuk misrule that the First Crusade was preached by an invigorated Papacy in 1095. But the idea that this enterprise was purely pious has long been dispelled. Political intrigue, commercial opportunism, love of adventure—many and potent were the material motives. Nevertheless, the Crusader goal and watchword was Jerusalem, not the merchandise of Beirut and the historian William of Tyre, who was no sentimentalist, wrote that as the knights came within sight of the city's walls they lifted their hands to heaven, flung off their shoes and kissed the dust where they knelt.

Ironically, the city was no longer in Seljuk hands. The Fatimid rulers of Egypt, a quixotic but more cultured enemy, had recovered Jerusalem the year before and had garrisoned it strongly with Arab and Sudanese troops. The Crusaders camped opposite the vulnerable northern walls, as Titus had done 1,000 years earlier. They numbered only 12,000 foot soldiers and some 1,300 knights, but their leaders were to pass into legend— Godfrey de Bouillon, embodiment of the chivalric ideal; the cold and haughty Baldwin; Raymond of Toulouse, civilized, enigmatic, vain; Robert of Normandy, eldest son of William the Conqueror; and the boorish and truculent Tancred, who had already seized Bethlehem.

For 40 days their siege proved fruitless. Their food and water dwindled, and a Muslim relief army was rumoured marching from Egypt. But on 15th July, 1099, the siege-tower of Godfrey de Bouillon lumbered across a filled-in ditch and grappled the walls. At noon, two Flemish knights and a picked storming-party established a bridgehead on the parapets, and the Damascus Gate was opened. The Muslims had no time to recover. Only the governor and his bodyguard reached the citadel and bartered for their lives. As for the rest, all afternoon and all night the Crusaders massacred men, women and children until none was left. The Jews took refuge in their chief synagogue and were burnt alive. Then, wrote William of Tyre, the soldiers "exchanged fresh clothes for those which were blood-stained, and walked barefoot with sighs and tears through the holy places of the city where the Saviour Jesus Christ had trodden as a man, and sweetly kissed the ground which his feet had touched".

Godfrey be Bouillon was elected lord of the kingdom of Jerusalem, but is said to have refused a crown of gold where his Saviour had worn a crown of thorns. Since the Crusaders had slain everyone in the city, and now forbade any Muslim or Jew to live there, they set about repopulating it with Syrian Christians and with Christians who had left before the siege and now returned. Among them, foreign quarters developed—German, Spanish, Hungarian, French, English—and the ancient Armenian community clung to the south-west. As today, Jerusalem became not a mercantile but an administrative and religious centre.

In this 14th-Century miniature, Crusader Godfrey de Bouillon is depicted twice— impassively crossing the Jordan (left) and beheading a camel with one blow. As ruler of Jerusalem, he consolidated his dominion over the Arabs with aggressive forays like this one.

It is in this period that detailed maps of the city appear for the first time, and the closeness to today's town is startling. You may walk down street after street where Crusader names—Street of the Furriers, Spanish Street, German Street, Street of the Repose—have vanished under Arabic; but their course is identical to the medieval routes. Even tiny lanes follow the old ways. Up and down the slopes they run in steep, mellow stairways, where the glide of long-robed women is coeval with any age.

Behind closed doors the courtyards of the houses are sometimes overhung by medieval vaults and arches. It was in Crusader times, too, that so many of Jerusalem's houses sprouted domes. From any small height you may see them froth among the rooftops, where some sweating Norman, short of roof-timber, demanded a high-domed room.

"The rooms keep warm in winter, too," a woman said, sweeping her doorstep with a bunch of chicken feathers. "How old is the dome? I don't know. It's been here always."

In the city's heart I thrust my way down the triple aisles of a long, vaulted bazaar. Its nooks and stalls, which Crusader burghers had rented from the Church or from city nobles, were hung now with sheepskin coats, Palestinian dresses, shoes and cheap gifts. Chinks in its roof shed down small squares of sunlight into the gloom. Here and there an inscribed T marked the estate of the Templars, and once a "Scta Anna" that of St. Anne's Church. Beside the Crusader "Street of Bad Cookery" I found the medieval herb market filled with butchers' stalls and the clash of iron-mongers. White hens, whose heads poked foolishly from tiers of cages, were being weighed, murdered, plucked and dismembered on the spot; and on every other booth, marble-eyed sheep's heads had been arranged in their blood, with a liquid heap of intestines and bowls full of goats' feet.

In their brief 88 years of tenure the Crusaders built as if their realm would last forever. You may still walk in the deep, quiet cloisters of their Latin-Saint-Mary, thick with lilac and ivy, or look above you on Calvary's chapel to see the last of their mosaics—a severe, time-darkened God, who lifts His hand in a vanished blessing.

In their day the Roman Catholic Church in the city stood as powerful as the monarchy of Jerusalem; its Patriarch, representing the Pope, was almost the Crusader king's equal. But the ancient Greek Orthodox Church, which had held sway before the Crusaders and to which the bulk of Arab Christians belonged, continued without influence beyond itself, old in the guile of the persecuted. Its churches were already turning inwards, effacing themselves. You may walk over today's Christian quarter and barely notice them. Sunk in the weight of other walls, rebuilt again and again on their old places, they open only a narrow doorway on a courtyard of jasmine or lemon trees. In the shrine beyond, you stand under the tattered glory of a half-forsaken Byzantium. A few lamps hang from vaults. An iconostasis gathers cobwebs. Musty cats sleep in the window.

The domes of houses bubble up over the Arab
quarter in the Old City. Rising above them
are the black tips of a few cypress trees, and—
a recent growth—a forest of television aerials.

But while the Greek Church bided its time, another, unique power grew up in the Crusader kingdom: that of the soldier-monks, the Knights Templar and Hospitaller. They left their mark in Jerusalem close to the Church of the Holy Sepulchre, where dense lanes spill into emptiness. Wide, short streets criss-cross one another in sterile ambiguity. A pompous Turkish architecture appears. This area, called Muristan, "the Infirmary", together with the near-by Church of St. John, remembers in its name the headquarters of the Knights of St. John of the Hospital. Originally merchants from Amalfi, who owned a hospital here before the First Crusade, they tended the wounded after the city was won, and so many of their patients joined the Order that it grew into a powerful military brotherhood. Vowed to poverty, chastity and obedience, the Knights Hospitaller, with the Knights Templar, became the spine of the Crusader body, and were soon to man half the castles of the kingdom against the rising Muslim sea.

Their quarter swelled with bazaars and a caravanserai, and after the Hospitallers had left Jerusalem the Arabs kept their hospital in use. Even in the 17th Century, wrote a pilgrim, "one sees still their infirmaries, and other rooms, but everything is abandoned, and nobody appears to live there". These remains were demolished, and long afterwards the present wide streets were laid, in the hope that Kaiser Wilhelm, on his state visit in 1893, might roll in a carriage from the Jaffa Gate to the Lutheran church. But luckily funds ran out and the weird streets were left unconnected to anything wider than a footway. They have never been touched by a wheel.

The Knights Templar had harsher beginnings. A mere eight men at first, they patrolled the Jaffa road to safeguard pilgrims, wearing with their armour only such tattered garments as they were given. But in 1124 they were granted as a palace the Aqsa Mosque in the Temple area. In contrast to the black mantle and white cross of the Hospitallers, they wore the white cloak and red cross under whose sign some 20,000 of them were to die before the kingdom of Jerusalem was reconquered by the Muslims.

West of the Aqsa Mosque they built a school of arms, that is now turned to the gentler ritual of a woman's mosque. And underground, in the huge Herodian vaults where their rock-hewn troughs and tethering-holes remain, they stabled the horses that were the nightmare of their enemies: chargers sometimes 17 hands high, trained to bite, butt and kick. You may see the Gothic gate, immured now, where the horses were led in and out with their attendant hacks and mules, and in that fetid silence feel again the awesomeness of these men: myrmidons of Christ, unwashed and uncouth, to whom bloodshed was a sacrament.

Yet sometimes it must have seemed as if peace, not battle, would overcome the Crusaders. A second generation grew up that had never known the European motherland, and intermarried with the local Christians and began to live like them. The royal court in Jerusalem grew used to the sight of native doctors and savants. The Crusader king himself gave audience cross-legged on his divan, dressed in a gold burnous, and the knights, discarding their European woollens, walked in the long coolness of silk and damask, wore shoes with tilted points, and lavish turbans. In Europe a baron might go unwashed from one year to the next, but the lords of Jerusalem were soon lolling in perfumed baths and drinking Damascus wines from goblets of arabesqued silver.

"We have already forgotten the places of our birth," wrote a chronicler, "they have become unknown to many of us or, at least, are unmentioned. Some already possess horses and servants here which they have received through inheritance. Some have taken wives not merely of their own people but Syrians, Armenians or even Saracens who have received the grace of baptism. Consider, I pray, and reflect how in our time God has transferred the West into the East. For we who were Occidentals now have been made Orientals."

Many of the women went veiled, if only to protect their heavily-painted complexions from the sun. Their robes and short Eastern tunics were embroidered in gold and even jewels. They developed a peculiar mincing gait and admired themselves in glass mirrors, unknown to Europe. They seem, all in all, to have been rather silly. The half-caste *poulanis*, like the Muslims, locked up their minx-like wives, who had a reputation for flirting and witchcraft; and the houses of the wealthy began to spread around fountained courts, like those of Saracen emirs, and employed furniture of a delicacy undreamt of in the North.

Rude parvenus from Europe were outraged by all this, and there was constant tension between the experienced urbanity of the older settlers and the fervid narrowness of the new. War against the Muslims, meanwhile, was never far away. Disease was rampant, and few lived to be old. In retrospect the people's luxury seems to have been carried with a neurotic frivolity into the abyss.

Only their buildings lasted. In the garden of the White Fathers near St. Stephen's Gate, the Church of St. Anne stands as it was built eight and a half centuries ago. After the pretension of other Christian shrines, after so much gaudy worship, this solemn church confronts the eye with the starkness of a winter tree. In its façade the arches of door and windows stand high and small, as in a fortress. Nothing disturbs its austerity.

Inside, barely a trace of ornament is left. The church was raised above an older crypt—the traditional birthplace of the Virgin Mary—and endowed richly by the wife of Baldwin I, the greatest of Crusader kings. Saladin, the Muslim leader who seized Jerusalem back from the Christians, turned it into a religious school, and his inscription is still above the door. But by the 18th Century the place had been abandoned and was reputedly haunted. Then the Ottoman governor quartered his cavalry in the aisles. The church became so sunk in refuse that a man could walk over the top of it. Only after the Crimean War did Napoleon III accept it as a gift of the sultan; soon

Built in the 12th Century, the plain and lofty Romanesque Church of St. Anne, in the north-east quarter of the Old City, is the only Crusader church in Jerusalem to survive substantially unaltered. Used as stables by the Turks, it was rededicated as a church in 1878.

afterwards he gave it to the White Fathers, restored to the serene, fortified style of the Romanesque—the loveliest church in Jerusalem.

With it the White Fathers inherited another priceless place only a few yards away: an ancient pool whose waters, now and then, were mysteriously troubled. In classical time a miscellany of pagan gods was worshipped here, and the healing basins carved from the rock by their devotees can still be seen. Even before Christ's time a wall divided this reservoir in two, one part filling with rainwater, the other with a strangely blood-coloured water that gave rise to legends.

"There is at Jerusalem", says St. John's Gospel, "by the sheep market a pool, which is called in the Hebrew tongue Bethesda. . . . In these lay a great multitude of impotent folk, of blind, halt, withered, waiting for the moving of the waters. For an angel went down at a certain season into the pool, and troubled the water: whosoever then first after the troubling of the water stepped in was made whole of whatsoever disease he had."

Here Jesus found a man who had been competing in this grotesque handicap race for 38 years, and with a few words, says the Gospel, healed him. Today the pool, long abandoned by its angel, is heaped with the debris of churches that once honoured and now defile it. A wrecked Crusader apse, barging shabbily into the sky, stands like a wraith of the serene St. Anne's above.

On 2nd October, 1187, 88 years after the Crusaders had reddened the city with the blood of her innocent, Saladin—the champion of Islam— reconquered Jerusalem after a siege of only 12 days; and with the clemency of strength he spared the inhabitants. No Crusader enterprise—

not even the brief rule of Frederick II early in the 13th Century—could return the holy city to Christendom. It fell under the power of Egypt, whose mercenary Tartars ravaged it, and after 1249, for more than two and a half centuries, it belonged to the Mamelukes in Cairo.

This aristocracy of former slaves (*mamluk* is Arabic for "owned") were mostly Turks and Circassians captured or bought in the markets of southern Russia and trained in the use of arms. Converts to Islam, they gained power in Egypt by numbers and ferocity. Their dynasties perpetuated themselves by a ruthless succession of the strongest. Distrustful and treacherous, the sultans recalled their city governors before they could properly govern, and were themselves assassinated as a matter of course—so often that the average reign of a Mameluke lasted less than six years.

At first their rule in Jerusalem was tolerant. The great Jewish scholar Nachmanides came to the city, and by the 15th Century others, fleeing persecution in Spain, had settled in the Jewish quarter of today. But the Christians—Greek, Roman Catholic and the innumerable lesser sects—fell into decline. Almost alone the Franciscans, whom the Muslims trusted for their mildness, bore the precarious privilege of guarding the holy places for the West, and of protecting the pilgrims who visited them.

The Crusaders, for all their faults, had organized their fiefs so prosperously that they became the envy of Muslims round about. The subtlety of the East may have bemused them, but the Arab could teach them nothing about administration, and as soon as their logical intelligence was withdrawn, the land began to decay. Jerusalem grew quieter. Its minorities hardened into the quarters that are still theirs: Christians in the north-west, Jews in the south, Armenians in the south-west.

But the Muslim sector, bulging around the Dome of the Rock, was endowed by the Mamelukes with religious schools and mosques. They seem to have held the city in distant benevolence. It became a haven for the pious and the scholar. Around the walls of the *Haram*, clustered about its gates or lining near-by streets, the façades of these tall and chilling monuments show gateways overhung by stalactite porches and joggled lintels. They are built in courses alternating red and white, black and white, but the use of vulnerable red marble and soft limestone has sometimes brought them close to disintegration.

A few of the most handsome and little-known streets are almost as the Mamelukes created them. Schools, mosques, palaces, tombs—they run in a dilapidated grandeur of dovetailed decorations, iron-bound doors, and fiercely barred windows. Here and there some blazon touches a personal chord—the cup of Tingiz, governor of Damascus, or the crossed mallets of an imperial polo-master—and their inscriptions are often pleasantly humble: "... given by the servant which longeth for Him, may He be exalted ..."

But if you should find one of the iron-bound doors unlocked, and walk inside, you discover the façade to be no more than a brave show. Behind it

A village woman wears her dowry on her head.

A conservatively attired Arab sits beside another in a modern T-shirt.

Red hair and blue eyes suggest Crusader blood.

This man's features and skin reveal an African heritage.

A young Arab still wears the traditional kaffiyeh.

# A Medley of Arabs

The basic Arab stock is Semitic, but Jerusalem's Arabs are part of a complex skein of many different threads. Other peoples, swept into contact with them as conquerors or concubines, soldiers or slaves, have contributed traits that are clearly discernible centuries later. And today the influence of the West is dramatically changing appearances by modifying the Arabs' customs and their traditional mode of dress.

On the furrowed skin of an elderly woman, dark tattooed patterns still show clearly. Today the practice of tattooing women's faces is rapidly dying out.

the disintegrating courts and rooms are inhabited by refugee families, who occupy them like rabbits, with their beds and stoves propped against the decorated walls, hastening decay. Everywhere the living lean upon the unacknowledged dead. Few can tell you who built what or who is buried where. Tombs lie in small courts piled with broken furniture and sheep's bones; and even the cenotaph of the Tartar chief who sacked Jerusalem rests without a curse in the dust of an old library.

These mosque-schools produced piety rather than thought. Unnoticeably, religion was corroding. It is an idea deep in Islam that truth is to be found in the community, heresy in the individual. And it seems that men in these hard times, forgetting that their own truth began as heresy, retired into the comfort of tradition and sealed their own tomb.

Yet always there were the unsatisfied, the mystics of Islam, the Sufis, who interpreted the Koran after their own fashion and by dance or ecstacy or contemplation tried to unite their spirit with Divinity. Many groups flourished in Mameluke times; but a few years ago, of all this legacy, only the tiny sect of Nachsbandiyeh was left in the city. This group, perhaps the most ancient of Sufi orders, was cradled in Turkestan and Persia, and had once acted as peacemaker among the descendants of Tamerlane. But its sheikh in Jerusalem, a man of courteous dignity, had told me six years before that the sect was dying, and that even his son would not carry on his ways.

I looked for him again. He was not in the café by his house. Instead I saw a young man with the slender-boned face of a Persian. When I asked for the sheikh, his features seemed to droop into his beard, but his eyes fixed me with a sad interest.

"My father died eight months ago. Did you know him?"

We sat at one of the tables and talked. The son had been in the United States as a student for three years before his father died, but as soon as he heard, he said, something happened inside him. He came back. "I started looking at myself. I missed him not just as a father, but as a leader and a friend."

I said: "I thought him a fine man." The dead often make us lie, but I could say this truthfully.

"He used to sit and teach me, but I never paid attention." The youth laid a long, melancholy hand against his face. He looked like a sultan from a Persian miniature. "I was more interested in films and girls then. But now that he's dead, what he taught comes back into my mind. He left writings behind him too. I've been reading what he wrote, over and over. Sometimes I don't understand, sometimes I do. But now I've grown up, and I find I can't let go my past."

What happened, I asked, to his father's sect?

It had seemed full of very old men, he said, even in his childhood. Some 20 of them had come with his grandfather from southern Russia after the First World War, and had buttressed a dwindling fraternity in Jerusalem.

"And now we've dwindled again. A few still speak Turco-Persian—it's a dialect our ancestors brought with them; but we've forgotten how to pray. Now that my father is dead, even the Muslim authorities won't recognize us any more. And my friends think I'm mad to go on studying the way." He smiled faintly. "In fact, I'm alone."

It was hard, he said, to begin from nowhere. Sometimes he would go and sit by his father's grave, as if asking for help; his father was buried in the house of a past follower.

Only one of the old Sufis was left. We found him sitting on an unmade bed in a sordid room, with his paralysed foot curled under him. He could remember fighting in the last war between Russia and the Muslims of Turkestan as a man already in his forties. It was a war in which both his sons had been killed. One had been 22, and I calculated by this that the Sufi must be close on 100 years old. But his body sat indecipherable in blankets, and his face was the ageless moon of the Tartars, immemorial people of the Steppes, the heart of Asia.

He offered us coffee, which he could not move to make. We refused gently and backed outside again into the too-bright sun. The youth said: "He is all that's left."

He took me to the sect's tiny mosque, an empty room glazed in dust. "At the end my father had only two followers. They would sit here by the light of a candle. At first he would call upon the names of God and read the Koran. In front of him where he knelt were 12 round pebbles. One by one, as the prayers continued, he would gather the pebbles into his hands and in these stages would draw nearer his goal, until he felt the names of God in his heart." He watched me intensely as he spoke. His eyes held the same liquid brilliance that I remembered in the sheikh, but set in a virgin face. "And when they had finished, and the last stone was gathered, they knew that God was with them. Something was there in their veins, in their mind, in their heart. Prayer, you see, is not of the mouth only. Your blood must pray with you. Even I understand sometimes . . ."

I walked home along the Mameluke walls, thinking of the Sufis who had thronged the older colleges, those who had studied in the Kankah or in the restful Dawadariyya, or who had whirled into mystic dance in the old Crusader church of St. Agnes, now a mosque. If it is comforting to think, with Islam, that the belief of the many enshrines a truth, it is sobering to realize that all the richness of this tradition in the city, all that multiple generations cherished and believed real, has shrunk to a trickle: a youth too young to inherit, and a sage too old to bequeath.

Early in the 16th Century the Ottoman Turks, spreading south after they had gobbled up the Byzantine Empire, found the Mamelukes at their mercy. The dynasty of slave-kings had grown effete with the centuries. Its provinces were poverty-stricken and its armies moribund. In 1517 Sultan

Suleiman the Magnificent, attended by two courtiers in this Turkish miniature, ruled Jerusalem from 1520 to 1566. The last of the great sultans, he beautified the city in many ways, before three centuries of decay and corruption closed over it.

Selim the Grim moved against them with the finest soldiery in the world, whereas the Mamelukes had scarcely seen artillery before. Against this magic even courage was useless, and their own sultan fell dead of apoplexy on the battlefield.

Jerusalem's walls had long ago crumbled, and by now its inhabitants numbered fewer than 4,000 families. It succumbed without a battle; its people had little worth defending. The savage sultan passed it by on the way to more distant victories, and not until the reign of his son, Suleiman the Magnificent, did the city feel the brief and benign touch of the Ottoman rule before it sank to its dotage. For several years after 1532, Suleiman repaired the aqueducts and dams and constructed his elegant fountains, which no longer flow.

Above all, he constructed the walls, which still suffocate and glorify the town. A tale runs that they were built by two brothers, architects who started in the west and circled away out of each other's sight for seven years, until their ramparts met at St. Stephen's Gate; but because they had excluded the Tomb of David from their wall's protection, says the legend, the sultan hanged them, and buried them near the Citadel, where you may see their graves nestled together under a fig tree.

This huge enceinte, completed in 1541 along the boundaries of the Roman and Crusader city, is a gesture of prestige rather than of defence. Suleiman, who owned the most modern gunnery of his time, must have known the battlements' limitations while he raised them—within the wider walls of an empire that already straddled the ancient world.

Stones of a soft pale grey, they crown the slope above the Kidron valley almost serenely; but across the western ridge they sharpen into towers: a savage discipline of spurs and angles. Inside the city, on airless summer days, you can feel the walls' strength squeezing the place dry. The crushed souks, the beetling houses, the threadlike lanes seem all to lie in the coils of a monstrous python, which at any moment will tense and the whole city crack and expire with a gasp.

Even the entranceways are low and deep, except where the Jaffa Gate was breached for Kaiser Wilhelm's state visit. The Damascus Gate, studded with the ends of fake columns and capped by frivolous crenellations, is less a bastion of power than a symbol of it, an architectural trumpet-blast.

But now the walls protect the city in a more personal way. They defend it from itself. No highway, no pylon, no office block has penetrated their stern ring. Outside, the world may go the ugly way of convenience. Inside lives a subtler and less explicable value, and the walls are its guardians, shielding not only the charm and squalor of the past, but the religious talismans of half mankind.

Suleiman was the last of the great sultans. After him came a stagnation so long and utter as to break the soul of any race or city. By the start of the 16th Century the whole balance of the Western world was altering momentously. New maritime powers—Spain, Portugal, England, Holland —were charting the seaway to the East around Africa, and discovering the Americas. Little by little the land routes of Asia emptied. The Mediterranean itself became a backwater, and its ancient countries sank into torpor.

Jerusalem shared the fate of all the Ottoman Empire. Its people were bled by taxes that spiralled with the greed of the local pasha, and the peasantry was soon reduced to serfdom, crippled by debts that were passed from generation to generation. The countryside, ravaged by the vendettas of feudal landlords, became eroded into a scrubland fit only for nomads. And while both government and justice depended on bribery, the militia was little more than a mounted brigandry called Bashi Bazouks, who were paid six shillings and eightpence a year plus pillaging, and recruited new members by kidnapping peasants.

As early as the 17th Century, visitors recorded that three-quarters of Jerusalem's houses were crumbling away uninhabited. A hundred years ago Chateaubriand, Flaubert and many others left pictures of the city's later misery and moral decay. "We were seated all day in front of the principle gates of Jerusalem," wrote Lamartine; "we made the circuit of the walls in passing before all its other gates. No one entered, no one came out; the beggar even was not seated in the gateway; the sentinel did not show himself on its post . . . We saw but four funeral parties issue in silence from the Damascus Gate."

Inside this dying monastery of a city, nothing new was built. Instead the old was patched and shored up above the compacted layers of its centuries, while deserted houses became ruins, ruins became dust. When street-workers dig to lay waterpipes or sewers, you may see how deep these man-made strata go. Even now the whole city is propped upon itself in an eternal convalescence. It interlocks, overlaps, undermines. The meanest wall may incorporate 20 ages. During four Ottoman centuries faiths, customs and buildings alike were embalmed in their own decay: a mouldering museum on which the 20th Century was suddenly to cast covetous eyes.

# 8

# The Mandate and After

When the British General Allenby entered the Old City on foot in December 1917—the first Western conqueror since the Crusader Godfrey de Bouillon—he received the keys to the Holy Sepulchre and announced prosaically, *"Status quo."*

But if this gesture confirmed the future of the venerable church, it was to be true of little else. And much of today's Jerusalem, a city many times larger than the Old City, is a product of the Western influence that the British accelerated. The Mandate ushered in a new era. The First World War was over. Almost at a touch, it seemed, the riddled edifice of the Ottoman Empire had come crashing down, leaving the entire Middle East to be parcelled among those powers that laid claim to it by conquest or tradition. Betraying an earlier promise to the Arabs, the British agreed to French control of both Syria and the Lebanon, and themselves extended their mandate over Palestine. Here, by the Balfour Declaration of 1917, the British government favoured a national home for the Jews, provided the rights of its other inhabitants were not prejudiced; and this famous document—conceived in a time when nothing, to the European eye, forbade the slow growth of a fruitful Jewish presence in the country—was to become the legal cornerstone of a new nation.

By this time Jewish immigration had enormously increased. As early as 1839 the community in Jerusalem stood at 5,000, and by the late 19th Century it had swelled to a majority in the city. The older groups of Sephardim, those from the East and the southern Mediterranean, were overtaken by Ashkenazim, the Jews from northern Europe, and this concentration in their holy city reflected a deepened religious idealism. In 1860 the British Jew Sir Moses Montefiore started to build the quarter of Yemin Moshe outside the walls: crenellated workshops and dormitories, with a windmill whose top has twice been shot off by Jordanian artillery and twice been replaced. This quarter was the first, tentative spreading westward of the Jewish townspeople, and remains as a monument to the hardiness of the first settlers venturing outside their old protections.

The Yemin Moshe quarter was followed by that of Mea Shearim. Settled by the ultra-orthodox, enclosed in walls, it still preserves the spirit of the 19th-Century pious. "Please do not antagonise our religious inhabitants by strolling through our streets in immodest clothing," runs a forbidding notice above one of the gates. Entering beneath it, I stepped back half a century into the ghettos of pre-war eastern Europe. Its few shops were gathered round a desultory fruit market, and wide, lonely streets ran among

**In a simple act of faith, and unaware of everything except her devotion, a Jewish woman kisses one of the rough stones of the Wailing Wall. A magnet for Jews from all over the world, the Wall attracts thousands of worshippers each year.**

silent houses. The beggar at the gate looked only as humble as everyone else. Strings of washing overhung the lanes, and from synagogues no grander than cottages came the half-moaning chant of the study and worship that never end.

The women have their heads shaved in accordance with the scriptures, and go about in wigs covered by headscarves. Most of the men wear the black robes of eastern Europe, where their centuries-long exile was endured: black stockings, shin-length black coats, black shoes. Under their wide-brimmed hats the wan faces seem already to look on eternity. Long side-locks fondle their necks or fly out in tufts, forever uncut as the Book of Leviticus demands.

Some of the men evoke an ancient glory. They are walking Methuselahs, their eyelids drooping impregnably over their fading gaze, and their beards bursting across their chests in grey rivers that sometimes reach the waist. Many of them are Hasidim, followers of a mysticism that was founded in the 18th-Century Ukraine. "The Holy One, blessed be He, requires the heart," quoted their founder. Upon this text he built a faith that in his day all but ignored the traditional stress on learning and replaced it with a spiritual reverence for the universe. Man, he taught, is a wave on the sea of God, yet every one a unique and precious creation. Some of the Hasidic leaders were known for their ecstatic visions and psychic powers; others probably were charlatans.

Among many others in the Mea Shearim quarter are the Mitnagdim of Lithuania who restored the Hasidim to the letter of the Law. There are the Dead Hasidim, who have lost their leader; and the Gerer Hasidim who are inspected by their rabbi as if they are a shabby infantry. The fanatic Hungarian Neturei Karta, "the Guardians of the City", hurl stones at any-one who dares to bicycle in their quarter on the Sabbath; their rabbi has for-bidden them to set eyes on the Wailing Wall until the coming of the Messiah.

Most of the orthodox of Mea Shearim are deeply pacifist. The Neturei Karta refuse so much as to handle the money or identity cards of Israel, whose existence they do not recognize; the true Israel, they say, will return with the Messiah, and they ritually spit when the present nation is mentioned, and fast on Independence Day. Slogans on the street walls equate the state of Israel with Nazism and show swastikas and stars of David grotesquely linked.

Behind the courtyard walls the half-heard murmur of voices is usually in Yiddish, for to many Hasidim, Hebrew is too sacred for conversation: it is God's tongue. The whole quarter is like a vast monastery. Its life is devoted to waiting, learning and self-correction. Its people, mostly poor, are supported by relatives or friends in other parts of Israel and in far-away countries. Cowled in white prayer-shawls before the glimmering candles of the synagogues, or praying alone in the quiet of their houses, the people are a sacrifice, from birth to death, to their fathers' law.

Tiny candles glimmer in the grim Chamber of the Holocaust, with its reconstructions of Nazi crematory ovens—a memorial to the millions of Jews murdered during the Second World War. It stands on Mount Zion to the south of the Old City, among monuments of earlier ages.

During the quarter century after 1875, while Mea Shearim was establishing itself, the Jewish population of Jerusalem swelled to 30,000. In 1897 the World Zionist Organization, founded under the Austrian Jew, Theodor Herzl, gave new shape and impetus to the yearnings of the Jews. A visionary who prophesied a Jewish state long before it came to be, Herzl envisaged this state as a refuge rather than a return—he even considered a tract of East Africa when it was offered by the British. But his followers refused, and in 1904 Herzl died, a saddened man. In 1949 his body was taken from Vienna and buried in Jerusalem on the hill that bears his name.

By the time of the British capture of Jerusalem in 1917, the tragic momentum of Arab nationalism and Zionist return was already building up. The 55,000 Jews in Jerusalem outnumbered all others of their people in Palestine, and it was on the city that the minds of both Jew and Arab focused, with religious passion and political anxiety. Every issue was more sensitive here, every incident more meaningful.

As early as 1920, riots broke out between Jew and Arab. So charged with tension had the city become by 1928 that when the Jews set up a small canvas screen to separate the sexes at the Wailing Wall, the Muslims protested that their sacred precincts on the Temple site were endangered. A British policeman removed the screen; the Jews complained to the League of Nations. And the dispute erupted into violence in 1929. This time more than 200 people were killed.

By now time was running out. Against a background of intensifying assassinations and strikes, the Arabs cried despairingly to the British for democratic government, accompanied by a prohibition of land sales and an end to Jewish immigration. But in Europe, Nazism was rising. Heightened persecution in Poland and Germany, and the reluctance of other nations to accept them, turned the Jews' eyes to Palestine as their only hope of a dignified freedom. Immigration, both legal and illegal, soared. The British could not stem it. Almost to the last they hoped to convert Arab and Jewish frictions into harmony. But by the end of 1936, the Mufti of Jerusalem, Amin al-Husseini, had organised a guerilla army in the hills, and turned it on his Muslim opponents as well as on the British and Jews. Against this terrorism the Jewish Irgun and Stern gang retaliated in kind.

Yet throughout these sombre years, Jerusalem was living anew. The British were active in fostering Arab education, and the Old City received public health services and fresh water. A big tourist industry grew up. North of the walls, handsome Arab suburbs thickened around the foreign and missionary institutions. Even today this quarter keeps a quiet, paternalistic charm, its buildings deep in gardens. The old schools, institutes, libraries and consulates succeed one another along its streets behind high walls.

The near-by slopes are scattered with ancient cemeteries, and the graves of Saladin's warriors. Here the British General Gordon, who was to die a hero's death at Khartoum in 1885, thought he had found the true

## Vignettes at the Wall

Since the 1967 War, when the Wailing Wall came back into their possession after it had been in Jordanian hands for 19 years, thousands of Jews have made the most of their good fortune. The intense emotional experience of the actual retaking of the Wall from the Jordanians, when Israeli soldiers wept as they touched the rough stones, has given place to a relaxed sense of ownership, of being "at home" by the ancient Wall. And thus on the enormous pavement spreading in front of it, dozens of little dramas are played out each day, some of a deeply-moving character, some as light or humorous as the vignettes recorded here—all testimony in one way or another to the living response that the eternal Wall continues to evoke from the Jewish people.

A mother reaches from the woman's side to comfort her son.

Stationed in the men's section to give out ritual skull-caps to those who need them, an official drowses in his glass booth.

Impatient at a dearth of prayer tables, this man has requisitioned a cart to bring one to his waiting congregation.

Calvary, and even a rival Sepulchre of Christ now lies in the piety of its gardens, so tranquil that one desires to believe in it. Here, too, stands the Dominican convent of St. Stephen, cradle of scholars. And to the east the Rockefeller family has built the Palestine Archaeological Museum to house a brilliance of riches ranging from the 100,000 year old Galilee Skull to the madcap decorations of the Arab palace at Jericho.

But west of the walled city, the older Jewish settlements have not remained so self-contained. Most have been engulfed by new arrivals. Jews came not only from a darkening central Europe, but also from Morocco, and even from Bokhara in southern Russia—kingly men who walk in striped robes and wear fur-lined hats.

In retrospect, it seems that by 1944 the situation was too steeped in blood to be retrieved. Soon the British, at a loss for any way to solve the problem, felt the brunt of Jewish bitterness. Jerusalem, inevitably, was the centre of the cruellest incidents, which measured the Jews' deepening disillusion with the Mandate. At the end of 1945 the police headquarters was blown up. In 1946 came the destruction of a wing of the King David Hotel, whose restored bulk still stands out in the skyline of the western city. More than a hundred army personnel and senior secretariat were killed.

Many ordinary Jews and Arabs still lived in the city side by side, yet neither they nor their leaders could understand each other's people in the heat of their emotions. Slowly they separated until the Jew, afraid that once again he was to lose the cherished land and city of his faith, stood in clear opposition to the Muslim, fearful for the home that had been his for 13 centuries. In May 1948, as the British surrendered their Mandate in despair, the waiting refugees poured out of a war-exhausted Europe into the Promised Land, and the armies of the Arab League closed in.

Again Jerusalem was under seige. Ever since January of that year, the city, a Jewish island in an Arab sea, had been heavily beleaguered. The twisting hill road from Tel Aviv to Jerusalem, perfect for ambush, was the only artery by which the Jews could be fed with arms and provisions. For a few days in April the Haganah irregular Jewish forces cleared the road and brought in supplies—the burnt-out husks of their convoys can still be seen. Then the ring was closed, and as of old the city fought against itself.

While the heavily-populated western town was able to hold its own against the Arab Legion and against Egyptian irregulars in the south, the inhabitants in the old Jewish quarter within the walls were few and mostly elderly. Eighty Haganah stiffened their ranks, but they had little ammunition; they were isolated from western Jerusalem—itself cut off—and gravely outnumbered.

"I managed to get in as a chaplain to our people," a resolute-looking rabbi told me. "But with so few defending—we never had more than 400 fighters—I had to take my place under arms. I remember clearly the day the British buffer troops evacuated—a Friday afternoon on 14th May—the

Among the relics of the British Mandate period that survive in Israel are a few red letter boxes, incongruously marked with the insignia of George V. Some are forlornly out of action, like this one, while others are still used.

Scottish soldiers leaving with bagpipes through the streets; a strange sight to us. The minute they marched out, war started.

"We had desperately few arms, but we took our two machine-guns and fired them from different posts, as if we had 40. We battled at every corner, over every stone. They would attack twice a day, morning and afternoon. They drove us back house by house. Yet all the time we had a mystical idea that we'd be saved. There was a feeling of redemption, as if our country was on its way. As if out of this agony a new child was being born—Israel.

"On the fourth day I was waiting with a sten-gun for the wave of their attack—they used to come in after the shelling. We had to stand in this shelling for about ten minutes waiting for them to come. Suddenly a terrible pain shot through my whole body. And I felt an odd surprise. My last memory was of clouds of dust from the exploded shell, and of being lifted on a stretcher. A long time later I woke up in our provisional hospital; just a room with 50 people in it. I still don't have the use of my left foot. It was four weeks before it was operated on. By then it was gangrenous.

"By the last day of battle we had only 36 soldiers left in the line. All the rest were dead, or wounded like myself. All through the siege there were moments of great sadness, but the worst was when our commander came into the hospital and said simply: We're surrendering. We were all against his decision. We wanted to go on until the end. But looking back on it now, I think he had no choice. There were fourteen hundred civilians packed into underground synagogues in the old city, and the enemy bren-guns were aimed at their doors.

"After our surrender the Arab mob moved in. From the hospital we could hear the waves of them reaching towards us. The Arab Legion and the Red Cross evacuated us just before they came running in for loot. I remember their roar and the fires flickering above the synagogues. We had to hobble in our casts to the safety of the Armenian monastery.

"Later we were marched through the Old City to St. Stephen's Gate, where a convoy was waiting to take us to Jordan. It was like a Roman victory parade. The people were howling. I was the last Jew to be carried out of the Old City—on a stretcher. Somebody came at me with a gun, but an Arab Legionary knocked it away. And all we could hear was the terrible cry of the crowd: 'Deir Yassin! Deir Yassin!'—the name of the Arab village which Jewish irregulars had exterminated."

On the ceasefire between Israel and the Arab states early in 1949, the Old City still belonged to the Jordanians, the new to the Israelis. An armistice line wobbled between them north to south, leaving a Jewish garrison on Mount Zion to shoot at Jordanians along the city wall, and Arab pill-boxes in the valley of Gehenna to machine-gun Zion. On Mount Scopus, where the Jews had founded a fine university and medical centre in 1925, an Israeli enclave was maintained by fortnightly convoys under United Nations supervision. The only link between the two cities was the Mandelbaum Gate, and even this was not a gate at all but simply a building once owned by a Mr. Mandelbaum, near which diplomatic personnel and occasional tourists gingerly crossed the line. The scar of the separation persists even now, not only in the disrupted souls of the people, but even in the rubble and ownerless olive trees that lie in a sordid blister between east and west.

So for 19 years Jerusalem was divided. It became, like Berlin, a dead-end city on either side. The Arabs cared for their part with an apprehensive pride, while in safety beyond the River Jordan it was Amman, the capital of Jordan, that mushroomed into unhappy life, filled with Arab refugees. Israel's part of Jerusalem also was quiet; to the west Tel Aviv became the rowdy city of the nation's international commerce, young and unlovely.

But all the time, against the Arab barricades of the Old City, the Israeli suburbs were piling up impatiently, partaking of the magic name *Yerushalayim*, but unable to touch any true part of the ancient and elusive city. West Jerusalem retains this air of hand-to-mouth buildings, of suburbs rushed into life to hold a surge of immigrants. It sprawls and scatters over its hills. Even in denser, older parts its character has been formed by a people used to fending for themselves and to building in small, personal ways. No bureaucratic palaces stare down. No fashionable boulevard glitters. Streets, people, houses keep an instant, practical vitality.

Here is the architecture of necessity. Its fine buildings are not its largest. But a facing of local limestone, compulsory as early as the Mandate, blends and softens all but skyscrapers, and the functional dwellings splashed over the hills are more homogeneous than those who live in them.

As deep a difference lies between old and young as between East and West. The old people have come from a harsh world, and may have suffered in mind as well as body. The young have grown up free and complete in their tradition. After 18 months of army service the girls move without grace. Heavy and nubile, they generally show the same soft limbs and rich, black hair as the Arab. The proportion of *sabras*—the native-born—in Jerusalem is greater than in any other city. They form a first generation, new in ethics, manners, sensibilities. Often impatient with the religious talk of their fathers, they are thrusting and even arrogant. They belong completely, and naturally, to the New Society. Yet with a difference: the sanctity, the specialness of the land and of the people still cling. History and faith forever welded, they remain—almost—religious without God. That is the meaning of *sabra*: a prickly fruit, spiky on the outside, soft within.

This ironic New Jerusalem, secular and proud, is still absorbed within the old. In so small a country, people have little choice of where to live. While businessmen go to Tel Aviv and industrialists to Haifa, the administrators and religious still gravitate to Jerusalem. The city grew up as a mosaic of ethnic and pious groups, and these remain. Its very street slang is a mulch of Hebrew, Yiddish, local Arabic, even the French of missions; its food reflects Arab and Turkish influences. The city lives conservatively, a little in secret. After 10 o'clock at night, the people used to say, you can see in the streets only dogs and Tel Avivans. Even culture is not very public. Compared to the coast, with its café life, the city has few public meeting-places: it seems to create quiet, reserved inhabitants.

But walking through the pleasant Jewish suburb of Rehavia, with its tended gardens and trees, I could feel that the people's insularity, like the old sectors themselves, was starting to blur. Many lived in flats in low-rise buildings. Names of international Jewry met the eye: "Rehov Disraeli", "Rehov Chopin", "Sir Charles Clore Hill Garden".

At the suburb's end the land drops westward, falling to long, Canaanite valleys. This immemorial country, dense in hills, is resistant to rigid town planning. The earliest and most imaginative Israeli scheme envisaged its slopes carpeted in housing above roads that went through fertile basins. And something of this vision now gathered in front of me. On one hill the Knesset, Israel's parliament, lay low in its young pine woods. On another the scattered geometry of the national museum looked across at the cubes and galleries of the Hebrew University. It is typical of the Israelis that when they lost their university and medical centre on Mount Scopus in 1948, they quickly rebuilt them in the west: the university larger, the hospital synagogue with windows by Chagall.

The Israel Museum, assembling its people's scattered history into order, is more characteristic of them still. A white porcelain dome covers its Dead Sea Scrolls—frail parchments of Isaiah illuminated as if on an altar. The people whisper around them. By such things they re-establish their identity and feel again their right to the land. Their archaeologists have become heroes. Every coin found, every stone unearthed from the biblical past is an act of remembrance, of reunion, even of piety.

Staring in dim light at the level and painstaking script, I recalled with faint surprise how the earliest New Testament manuscript, the *Codex Sinaiticus*, lies in the British Museum unnoticed. I shuffled around the scroll as if its text must yield some secret. Two Israeli soldiers, male and female, followed me around, he with one hand on his sten-gun, the other on the girl's waist. Our heads crammed together against the glass. But the letters on the parchment, exact and small as insects' work, remained unimaginably remote, scratched at a time when nothing but this talisman of scripture seemed important in the world at all.

# Sanctum of the Orthodox

**A bearded Hasid lights Hanukah candles to symbolize the re-dedication of the Temple after its desecration by Antiochus Epiphanes, over 2,000 years ago.**

In the northern part of Jerusalem lies the shabbily picturesque quarter of Mea Shearim, home of the Hasidim and other ultra-orthodox Jews. Begun in 1874 outside the walls of the Old City, it was built like a fortress, with its terraces and windows facing inwards. It is populated today almost entirely by east European Ashkenazi Jews. Retaining much of the dress, customs and speech of the 17th-Century ghetto, they are in theological conflict with the "blasphemous" life of the modern state of Israel. Here, in a community that does not tolerate disrespect for their traditions, daily life and the worship of God are intertwined, and the precepts and rules of conduct outlined in the Torah and the Talmud, the ancient books of law and learning, are strictly observed by all the members of the quarter, some to the point of fanaticism.

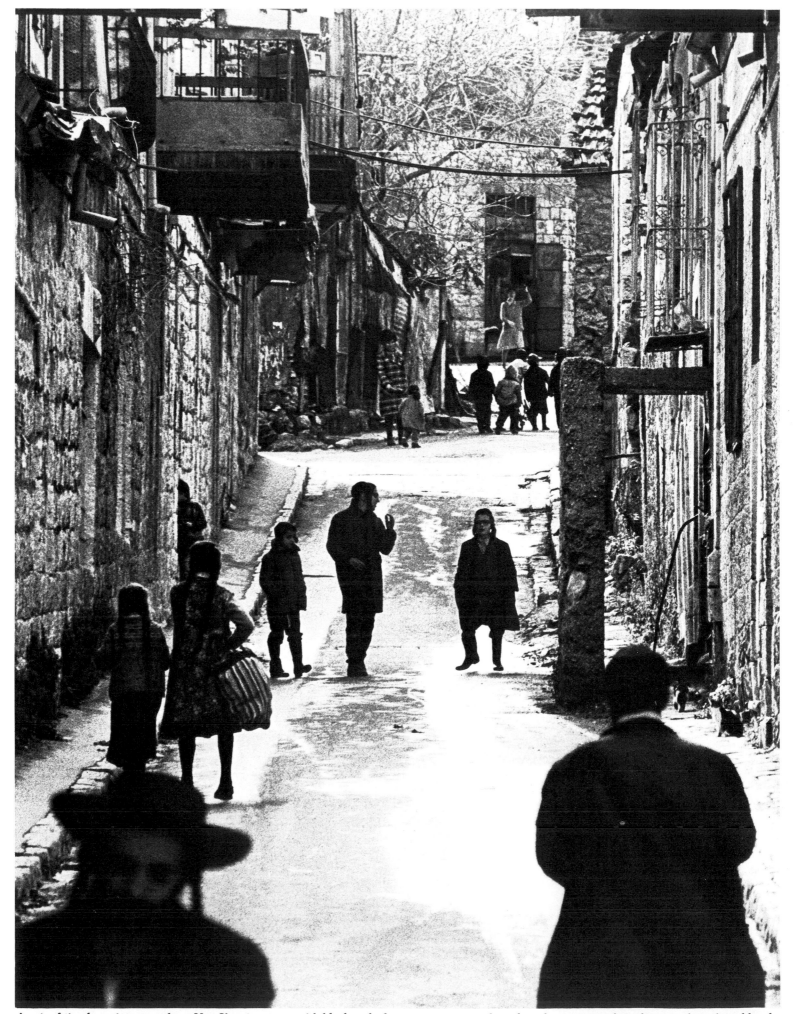

**An air of timeless piety pervades a Mea Shearim street, with black-garbed men in peiyot or side-curls and women wearing wigs over their shaved heads.**

A father, in long black coat, striped kaftan and wide-brimmed hat, steers his son to synagogue.

Under the watchful eye of their rabbi, the boys in a synagogue school sit at their desks, ready to interrupt their religious instruction for lunch.

**Although a page in his Talmud is torn, this rapt scholar can recite for his teacher the missing passages from memory after years of study.**

An elderly Hasid continues a lifetime's devotion by silently scrutinizing the Talmud. The Hasidim believe that such study helps bring them closer to God.

At a synagogue door two Hasidim speak Yiddish: many hold Hebrew too sacred for daily use.

Bending to ask after a crippled friend's well-being, a Hasid demonstrates the concern that members of the Mea Shearim community show for one another.

# 9

# The Return

On the morning of 5th June, 1967, while Israeli air strikes in Sinai were deciding the course of the Six-Day War, Jerusalem remained silent. Five days earlier, King Hussein and President Nasser had reached a private agreement, but Israel believed that Jordan was too vulnerable to attack her, and the Jewish city was defended only by a brigade of elderly reservists. Its people went about their business, and the children were even at school.

But at 10.15 that morning the first mortar bombs fell on the city, and soon artillery had opened fire all along the line. The Israelis quickly moved up tanks from the coast, and deflected a brigade of young paratroopers who were about to be airlifted to Sinai. Israeli Army Headquarters began to plan the assault that was to bring them as victors to Old Jerusalem. The armoured brigade would push through the Jordanian positions west of the outskirts, until it could round on the city from the north, while the paratroopers were ordered to fight their way into suburbs close to the walls and so relieve the beleaguered Mount Scopus.

At this time, with shells falling among them, the Jewish citizens of Jerusalem could only guess at what was happening. "Towards nightfall," a journalist told me, "the Jordanian bombardment intensified. From my roof I could see the mortar shells raining on Scopus. That night the telephone and lights were cut off. Down in our air-raid shelter was another journalist, an orthodox rabbi and an ex-ambassador to Denmark, all crammed together in candlelight. When the shelling grew fiercer, the rabbi put on his prayer-shawl and started to pray. He was afraid. And of course we couldn't sleep. I ventured out at about one o'clock in the night, when the battle was very intense, and saw the whole horizon red from artillery and mortar-fire. Yet in between the explosions it was utterly quiet. There was no light. And the silence was almost more frightening than the guns. The stars were shining. There is a strange echo in those hills, too, and the explosions went on and on, their reverberations hollower and fainter."

All that night the battle north of Jerusalem was the closest fought and bloodiest of the war. The Israeli armoured brigade attacked on a five-mile front. The Egyptian air force, which was to have given the Jordanians cover, had been annihilated in Sinai, and the small but strongly entrenched units of the Arab Legion were left unsupported. The Israelis advanced painfully, picking out mines by hand in the fading light, until a rough path was cleared and the first position fell to their armour. By early morning they had captured the key hill above Jerusalem, lost it, recaptured it and at last stood astride the slopes that looked down upon the Old City.

**A young Israeli policewoman directing traffic in the heart of the new city of Jerusalem combines an air of command with a certain chic. She is a sabra, an Israeli-born and educated Jew.**

Meanwhile, at terrible cost, the paratroopers were advancing through the northern suburbs. The Jordanians lay ready behind barbed wire in a warren of rock-lined trenches and bunkers, with heavy machine guns, mortars and artillery. The paratroopers, illuminated in the flash of gunfire, were mowed down as they crossed the minefields. But their survivors blasted through five barbed wire fences, until they reached the trenches and pill-boxes, where the Jordanians fought them hand to hand until the end. Now, near the walls of the Old City, there stands a remarkable monument —raised by the Israeli soldiers to the courage of their Arab enemies. As for the Israelis, one company was left with only four men, another with seven.

They were faced at last by the high, grey walls of Suleiman the Magnificent, lined with snipers. Anyone who approached was shot, and all next day the battle lulled. "Towards evening," the journalist said, "I heard that the road through the Mandelbaum Gate had been opened for the first time in 19 years. That night I realized that they were going to take the Old City. And after midnight I heard the Israeli assault moving along the Kidron. They were battling for Gethsemane, but the Arab Legion ambushed them." This setback saved the Jordanians for a few hours more.

**The ornate outline of the upper portion of the Damascus Gate in the city's northern wall frames the silhouette of an armed Israeli soldier, on the alert after a warning of terrorist activity in the Muslim quarter.**

By dawn on 7th June the walled city was all but surrounded, and within a few hours the Mount of Olives, too, had fallen. From here, brazenly, the paratroopers assaulted the walls at their steepest. Their brigade commander, Mordechai Gur, raced beyond his own tanks in a half-track, and charged alone up the ascent to St. Stephen's Gate. Squeezing beyond a burning vehicle, he drove against the iron doors, burst them, jolted past a dazed Arab soldier, veered to the left and found himself on the Mount where 1900 years before, the Temple of his ancestors had been thrown down by the emperor Titus.

"We went in with an army column," said the journalist. "There were bodies by the Damascus Gate, and parts of bodies, and burning tanks and buses. We ran on foot through St. Stephen's Gate—the only one we could penetrate. Reaching the Temple Mount, in the late afternoon sun, was an awe-inspiring sight. We saw Israeli soldiers in full battle gear with radios. Some old Arab men were on the wall, shivering with fear. They were lined up to be searched; but they thought they were going to be shot. All the soldiers were running to the Wailing Wall. There was room in the cramped enclosure for no more than a couple of hundred. Many were wounded, crying like children, touching the stones. . . . "

Immediately upon its capture the area around the Wailing Wall was cleared of houses and turned to a white-paved emptiness. Now it is planned that the ground in front of the wall be lowered to its ancient level, while behind it ever-mounting terraces will reach to the newly-built Jewish quarter. Anything, perhaps, would be better than the blazing aridity of the present site. But the Wall, at heart, is a symbol of loss, the private grief of an outcast people. The shrine of a victorious nation it cannot be. As soon as it is glorified, I feel, it becomes grotesque, and to floodlight and terrace it is a contradiction, a lapse in feeling. Yet all schemes persist in turning its weeping into grandiloquence, while in truth it would be better left to the devotion of the orthodox, for whom Israel will not truly have returned until the Messiah brings her.

This points to a wider dilemma. During countless centuries the role of the Jew has been that of thinker, dissenter and rebel. His great religious duty was to preserve his people. But this traditional plight has little meaning in Israel. The Wandering Jew has long returned, and with his return both he and the world may be poorer. After so long troubling and inspiring the societies of others, he has reached his own society—and is unsure how it should be formed. Attainment is always loss. Where shall he go now?

"Returned?" echoed an atheist Israeli brusquely. "We haven't returned anywhere except to another oriental city." He sighed angrily, but did not look as hard as his words made him sound. "As for the Wall, what is it? A pile of stones. When I think that people were killed for that, I want to puke." Yet even his idealism was deeply Jewish, uncompromising—

Shoulder to shoulder, blocks of a new Jerusalem suburb reach upwards into a tranquil sky. Constructed on rolling hills to the north of the Old City, the development is occupied largely by recent immigrants.

the desire to build a New Jerusalem, if not between God and man, at least between man and his true state.

"We had a chance to raise a new society here," he said, "a decent democracy without religious cant—a freedom of the intellect and imagination. And instead we have these people dressed like scarecrows and moaning and banging their heads against the Wall."

"Are there many in Israel," I asked, "who feel as you do?"

"Perhaps not many, but more and more. Maybe eight per cent or so. I just don't know."

I remembered the red-haired rabbi I had met among the ruins of Mount Ophel. To him, too, the return of Israel to her Temple had been half disappointment. "It's not enough to gain a holy place," he said in his fastidious way, "unless you become holier by acquiring it. But the state of Israel chose to be a secular state. It could have been something great, but it refused the challenge. God is as near in any place as in the Temple. The problem is whether we are nearer to him." He paused, mopping his forehead. "The Hasidim have a question: Where is God? and they answer: God is found in the place where you let Him in. Every good deed is a sacrament. When the Temple is destroyed you have to create it in yourself, which is, of course, much harder."

"But some want physically to rebuild it?"

"Oh yes, certainly." He betrayed a wisp of a smile. "I've met orthodox who've studied the texts with such perfectibility that they'd be ready to serve in the Temple tomorrow. But what is the use? If the people don't participate with God, the place is deserted." His mouth soured in the fitful red beard. "The danger would be of raising another empty building."

It is partly as a symbol of their return that the Israelis are rebuilding the half-ruined Jewish quarter south of the Wailing Wall, which fell to the Arabs in 1948. Half the houses were still in ruins when I walked there. The Ramban, oldest of the synagogues, built in 1167; the great Hurva; the Bethel where the Cabbalists worshipped—all were shells, open to the sky, where a few Arab children scampered in and out, or stopped to gaze at me with ancient faces.

But around them every other ruin clinked with chisels, dripped and thudded with falling stones and plaster; and workmen were cantering their donkeys back and forth flamboyantly over the rubble-strewn spaces. Where rebuilding is complete, the lanes climb steeply among angled houses in rosy stone. It is a close, quiet quarter, as it used to be, with few windows, and needs only time to bring it back to life. Already the religious schools are filled with the susurration of learning. And doubtless many of the 3,000 to live there will be orthodox, although more secular Jews are being encouraged to settle. Nevertheless the place is in danger of becoming self-conscious, a quarter of empty *chic*. The houses are not given back to those who once owned them, but sold to any Israeli who can afford them.

The curved roof of the Shrine of the Book (top right) in the grounds of the Israel Museum copies the shape of the lids of earthenware jars in which the Dead Sea Scrolls were found. Some of the Scrolls are now displayed in glass cases inside the Shrine (below).

"I feel too much for this place even to ask for compensation," a woman said emotionally. She had bought back her old family home. "It is my childhood, my blood. And to me it is beautiful, the whole quarter." She showed me the vaulted rooms of the house, leading one into the other by arched entranceways. "You can't buy your emotions with money. My family owned this house for more than 200 years. My father was head of the Jewish community." Walking among the arches, over the small courtyard, she smiled like a girl: a face strangely free of wrinkles under greying hair. "In those days people were more religious than now. Churches, mosques and synagogues here were all jumbled together. We were surrounded by different neighbours too—Arabs upstairs and on one side, Armenians across the road. We used to play together as children and it never occurred to me to ask 'Is he a Jew?' 'Is she an Arab?' I wish, I believe, those times will come again."

But a more dramatic change is overtaking the city along its skyline. Where once it lay in a theatre of sculptural hills, whose rocks and soils and shrubs reflected its own hard beauty, its horizons now are choking with flat-blocks rushed up, it has been said, "for urgent political reasons". The Israeli government is circling the old, largely Arab city in suburbs settled with 150,000 Israelis on expropriated Arab land—"a plan with a Jewish goal", an Israeli housing minister said. The act is fraught with complications. In 1967 Israel broke with the Geneva Convention by annexing Jerusalem, although no state among the United Nations supported the decision. It was the logical move of a people who had always believed in their own destiny and acted alone: a statement of faith in themselves.

The buildings surround the city of God with its old and ugly truth, that politics and religion cannot disentwine. They fill the gently swelling stresses of its hills with the vertical thrust of a placeless modernity, with the glare of the new on the glow of the old.

And while the Israeli housing authority has plundered the hills, the Municipality had allowed high-rise projects to be built in the centre of west Jerusalem. As you ascend the Mount of Olives they erupt like nightmares behind the Old City, and their names should be recorded as mutilators of the most sacred city landscape in the world: the Omariyah, built on public land without permission; the Hilton, to the west; and most domineering of all, the Plaza Hotel, perched in this clear, foreshortening air high between the Aqsa Mosque and the Dome of the Rock.

The most angry complaints have been those of the Israeli public; and it is public pressure that has aborted some of officialdom's monsters, and cropped others. The failure of the Municipality—a body of hard-worked and devoted men—seems to have been in sensitivity and foresight. Chronically in debt, they allowed the desire for foreign currency and tourism to dim other values, and the charge that they are scarring the city they love has perturbed them. They recognize now—almost too late—that skyscrapers here are an anachronism, and plan to grade future buildings by altitude, with almost nothing taller than eight storeys. But many licences were granted years ago, so more nightmares are almost certain to arise. And the Israeli Housing Authority continues to lock up the Old City in concrete walls on every hill.

Jerusalem cries out uniquely for a tenderness towards the past, instead of a brash insistence on our own ephemeral needs. Man, says the Koran, loves the transitory but neglects the eternal.

There is a danger, too, in the attempts to "beautify" the Old City. For the city is already beautiful: not in a self-conscious Western way, but in a subtler, more natural mould. Here the disparity between West and East is strongest. The well-meant Israeli landscape park around the Old City is cosseting the place like a museum, while Arabs still work and inhabit it in feudal squalor. There is something ridiculous about terracing the Valley of Gehenna. For one culture the Old City is a symbol, a dream fulfilled. For the other, a roof and a job.

Perhaps it is ungracious to object to the landscape park; one wishes only that it was wider, and is deeply relieved by the Municipality's determination that the whole area of the Old City and the Mount of Olives, with other historic pockets scattered round it, should rest under a preservation order. There was no such security under Jordan.

Meanwhile, the Arab, who generally admires whatever is modern, has political, not aesthetic worries. His community of 70,000 is outnumbered by an escalating Jewish population of more than 220,000, and he feels himself swamped. The Muslim, in particular, is ill-equipped to respond vitally to such a challenge. Walking in the Old City, I watched him brooding among the cafés, his children in the streets, his women out of sight. The Renaissance of Europe, the Industrial Revolution passed him by. The great Muslim empires, which on one side had split over the Pyrenees and on the other beat at Vienna's gates, lie in tatters about him. He lives in their falling stones. The wealth of the Arab oil fields cannot reach him. Through his half-open doors you see no scenes from the Arabian Nights, but stone stairs twisting to darkness.

Even his own change may bewilder him. The aristocratic families—Nashashibi, Husseini, Alami—have ceased to dominate the civil and religious offices. Many have left. Arabs from Hebron, abrasive and crudely commercial, have elbowed their way into the minor trades. A new generation has grown up, of half-educated sons who reject their fathers' calling.

The Muslims of Jerusalem are more austere than most, more tenacious, perhaps more sceptical. Some were refugees from the newly-formed Israel of 1949. And all the old Arab qualities remain. The people are ever quixotically proud, yet yielding, secretive, mercurial. Facts and logic grow dim under the surge of their dreams and senses; truth lies in feeling. Yet the creative imagination is not theirs. Personable and clever, the Arab is the great individualist, who yet often lacks true individuality. His anarchy and limitations seem always the same.

Cut off from other Islamic lands—for the Mecca pilgrims can no longer pass through Jerusalem—the Muslims are isolated. Instead, the city is turned to the West, to an Israeli culture that is dynamic and exclusive. The Arab, even when ruled by his own, has no instinctive trust that he will not be corrupted and divided by this more powerful economy. Peace with Israel might be as great a danger as war with her, and the isolation of arms can be safer and more dignified. Now he is exposed.

The 11,000 Christian Arabs, with their traditions in commerce, are wealthier than the Muslims. They still live in the west around the Holy Sepulchre, in a higher and healthier quarter, closer to the gates where once the trade of the Mediterranean flowed. Because many follow the middle-class professions traditional to clever minorities—doctors, lawyers, clerks—they have suffered in the competitive and highly-taxed Israeli state, and some of them, with educated Muslims, are leaving.

The Christian churches are many, even among so few. The Orthodox Patriarch lives in Olympian state among a jumble of convents and courts, and claims succession from the bishops of Jerusalem since Hadrian's time. The Roman Catholics are protected not only by their Patriarch but by a pontifical delegate, and by the head of the Franciscans, who presides over the spreading jungle of the Terra Sancta convent. The Syrian Orthodox, whose faithful number barely a hundred, keep their quaint Church of St. Mark and still read their liturgy in Syriac, a language close to that of Christ.

To the south, the compound of the Armenians holds its churches and seminary, its treasury and library, in an oval of quiet walls. Its courts are half deserted. Here and there a cowled priest moves on his shadow; or a gaggle of women assembles where an old prophetess lives in a cell behind many doors, and interprets dreams.

The Armenians' Church of St. James, they say, stands over the corpse of St. James, the brother of Christ, brought here in the 4th Century from his grave in the Kidron valley. Beyond its Crusader nave, splashed with bright blue tiles, the altar rises in a golden conflagration of icons and monstrances. The place is filled with stories. The last queen and princess of Cilicia are buried under the northern aisle. In a chapel near by, it is said, lies the head of St. James the Great. And beyond, a priceless treasury holds the sceptre of King Hattun II of Armenia—a rod of pure amber almost a yard long—with a silken cope cut from the tent of Napoleon at Jaffa.

The Armenians, as in all the Levant, are jewellers, and their work is honest and delicate in a city where souvenirs are sold with no other merit than the name Jerusalem. Works of craftsmanship, let alone works of art, are rare. Until the end of Turkish times artist-pilgrims produced icons in

A donkey stands patiently in the rain, waiting for its load of petrol cans to be filled with kerosene. The fuel will be delivered to homes throughout the city to be used for cooking and heating: Jerusalem winters can be dismal.

return for their lodging, but these have disappeared from the market, and the satin voice of the shopkeeper who talks of "ancient pictures" is almost sure to be fraudulent. Blandly he will indicate a shelf stacked with grimed and corroded fakes, painted on to worm-eaten wood. Only if the tourist frowns and grumbles will the shopkeeper beckon from behind the counter and open a low cupboard. Behind it stand older, less decipherable icons. These too are fakes. Only then, if the tourist frowns harder, may he be conducted to the home of a family willing to sell its icons. And even then . . . "Paint them, put them in the fire, and they come up good as old!" a man confided to me. "The Franciscans do them here, and some of the Russian Orthodox . . . "

Many of the shops inside the Old City have flourished since Israeli rule. Their prices have soared. And so have wages. And so have taxes. Arab manual workers, some of whom cross into west Jerusalem for employment, are enjoying salaries that outweigh increased prices and taxation, and their families, often large, find that they can apply for allowances. It is the white collar workers, the employers and the landowners, in a society fiercely egalitarian beside that of Jordan, who find themselves less comfortable. But some of these, too, have begun to recover or to adapt.

"People don't complain so much about material things," an Arab told me: a man with dark, emphatic features standing in the doorway of his business. "A few of us are better off, certainly. But the Israelis won't win us that way. Even my dustman says he'd rather earn half of what he does and be free." The man bent his black eyes on me, suddenly hesitant. Was I, perhaps, an Israeli spy? He decided not. "If you've never lived under occupation you can't understand. But if we go, they take our houses. If we're outspoken, they deport us." He clasped his hands bitterly together, as if to prevent them tearing something. "None of us wants to leave here. Most of us would stay and eat dust in this country rather than leave."

"And the others?"

"Some have found it unbearable," he said curtly. "Others have lost their houses. Hundreds have been displaced from the Jerusalem area alone. In the old Moroccan and Jewish quarters, if they didn't move, their houses were all but bulldozed over them. And what were they paid in compensation?" He spat. "A pittance, a camel's ear. And how many were rehoused? Not one in 30. They had to fend for themselves. Even in the Jewish quarter most of the land had never belonged to Jews. It was rented by them from the Muslim religious trust." The man dashed his hand against his forehead as if he must be sweating. But his face was clear and drawn; only his eyes seemed to betray the anger of his people. "My own brother", he continued, "owned land which was expropriated against his will, and he was paid a fool's price for it."

"Didn't he fight?"

The man exploded with bitter laughter. "Fight? They just took it."

I looked down at my feet shuffling awkwardly on the pavement. "The Municipality is trying," I began. "You have new water, new drainage . . ."

"In exchange for our freedom they give us sewers!" he shouted.

Several passers-by turned to stare at us. The man thrust his angry hands behind his back, quieted himself with visible effort. "I'm not saying everything was good in the Jordanian time," he went on. "Everything is never good. And the Jordanian administration was corrupt. It took years to get anything done. If you wanted a new telephone or a car licence you had to ask Amman. Practically if you wanted to sneeze you had to ask Amman! But at least it was Arab, it was ours." He sighed vigorously. "But here we're second-class citizens. We can never thrive. The Israelis belong only to themselves. And slowly they're going to run over us."

His head jerked back towards the battlemented hills, white with their new flat-blocks. "Do you think Arabs live in those? No. Even if we were let in, we couldn't afford them." He started to drum the curb-stone with his foot. "But we have feelings which won't change. When our dignity is hurt, we never forget. You may see us living with these people on the surface, but no more than that. The blow has gone too deep. If the Israelis stay a hundred years we won't have drawn nearer to them one step."

The liberal and energetic Jewish mayor of Jerusalem, who has often stood up for its minorities, regarded such feelings as natural and perhaps inevitable. "The Arabs have a right to say what they think. Our policy has never been to absorb or integrate them. Our aim is only to coexist happily, and that will be hard enough." He spoke with voluble frankness from behind a laden desk. Coping with the condition of a wildly varied populace —Zionist, Arab, the fiercely religious, the belligerently secular, business-man, aesthetes—his mayoralty must be the most exacting on earth.

"We have to abolish any idea of a paternalistic Jewish attitude," he declared. "None of us wants it. In any case, each of us—Arab, Jew, Armenian, Catholic—feels superior to the rest. Jerusalem has always been a city of sects. And we'll go on respecting that. The failure of peace negotiations makes everything more difficult—the Arabs here are worried at being thought collaborators. But they're gradually taking more responsibility for their own affairs, and this is what we aim at."

When I carped at the explosion of high-rise building around the city, he jumped to his feet and took me to the window. "Look at those hills. What would you do with them?" We gazed south towards valleys touched with tentative suburbs. "Would you cover them all with low-rise buildings, or would you build higher and leave more open space? We're already turning valuable building sites into parklands around the western walls. That must be almost unique in any city centre." He paused and added moodily: "As to skyscrapers, we admit our mistakes. Some permits were granted before 1967, while we had no concept of a unified city. But the Arab complaints are mostly just emotional. The new flat-blocks were all built on grazing-

In one of new Jerusalem's main streets, afternoon sunlight gleams on the traffic which is thickening as rush-hour approaches. Buses belonging to the nationalized bus company loom over small European-built cars, and an Arab jaywalker nips between the vehicles.

land, which wasn't even under cultivation. It's true they'll house Jews. But the Arabs evacuated from the old Jewish quarter, who were many of them squatters from Jordanian times, are beginning to build houses for themselves now.

"As for the future, I don't envisage a rich town, but it will be better off than now, when we are still filled with refugee immigrants."

Compared to the civic problems of Haifa and Tel Aviv, those of Jerusalem are mountainous. Families are big and welfare expenditure high. Of the Jews, almost half the population is under 15 years of age. Among the Arabs only a quarter of the houses have baths; the people live, on average, more than two to each room. So welfare problems alone are sufficient for any municipality, without the deeper concerns of serving a city in which half the world claims a spiritual share.

If you walk now where Israeli and Arab pass each other in the Old City, you may see in their faces a lesson more profound than any propaganda. The euphoria of the Six-Day War has drained from the Jew; the battles of 1973 and later developments were less happy for him. Despite the increased frenzy and tensions of the city's life, its people—Arab and Israeli—are now starting to regard each other with the dry acceptance that can last for generations. They converse through a veil. The Arab shopkeeper smiles, bends, distantly tries to sell something. The Israeli bargains, departs. Nothing touches, nothing alters. The Eastern Jews are sometimes so close to the Arabs in looks and manner that they cannot be distinguished from them; but even they, coming as many do from hatred in Arab countries, may feel suspicious or vindictive. The Western Jew is patently different. He, to the Arab, is the ruler, the imperialist. The young Israeli-born push through the streets in the casual dress of the universal young. Nothing could be further from the image of the persecuted Jew. They live in a brazen and demanding world: a frontier generation. The army moulds them; and at university they have not time for dilettantism, only for getting qualified.

The Arab, to whom appearances matter, regards them with puzzled distaste. Traditionally Puritan, he looks askance at their free-loving and free-thinking. Yet paradoxically it may be this more liberal youth that promises eventual coexistence. Because the Arab young, too, are slowly sloughing off traditional ways; even their girls are losing their pampered look, and sometimes make their own decisions. There is, it seems, only one way of being modern. And it is the young, whatever the old may think of them, whose society is increasingly classless and nationless—a society of peace.

But the ancient ways prevail. The brutal fact is that for decades to come neither Arab nor Jew could relinquish Jerusalem without committing psychological suicide. Everything else is negotiable, but not this city. It stands like a rock in the path of peace. The Jew has traditionally relied on himself. His very faith binds him to his own, and the outside world has only ever betrayed him. After two millennia of exile and persecution he has returned in hardship to the country and the city of his soul, and nothing will tear him away.

But even as one looks with awe and admiration on the Jewish achievements, and feels the justice in their return, one sees the Muslim humiliation and loss, the wrenched souls of a people whom time has profoundly wronged. They, too, clung to Jerusalem, loved it and held it sacred, and their rights to the city are the natural ones of a continuous tenure over 13 centuries.

Paradoxically, the Jerusalem of Heaven has created its earthly opposite: a metropolis that has evoked more bloodshed than any other on earth. Although religion even here is waning, the fervour remains for this pitiless city: the symbol, the mystical identity.

"I saw a new heaven and a new earth," says the Revelation of St. John the Divine, "for the first heaven and the first earth were passed away; and there was no more sea. And I, John, saw the holy city, new Jerusalem, coming down from God out of heaven . . . And God shall wipe away all tears from their eyes; and there shall be no more death, neither sorrow, nor crying, neither shall there be any more pain: for the former things are passed away."

The earthly state is forever seen as a jumbled puzzle, whose pieces may be shuffled into perfection. There was once an ideal city. But somewhere, at some time, the formula was lost. Behind it, like a talisman, it has left its lonely gift: dissatisfaction. So that year by year, century by century, men find only limited perfections and temporary ends, and by these must redeem themselves in the face of whatever God is listening.

# Contrast and Unity

**Christianity's symbol stands tranquil in the Church of Dominus Flevit (above). It is also produced by the boxful for tourist consumption (left).**

Wherever you look in ancient or modern Jerusalem, chance juxtapositions speak of the complexities and contradictions of life in a city of many religions and cultures, where the record of a long past is being amended by the dramatic events of today's fast-moving world. Variety is visible on every hand—old and new, rich and poor, commercial and spiritual. Yet in such contrasts there can lurk an element of latent violence, as ragged beggars confront brocaded priests, gleaming skyscrapers of steel, stone and glass crowd in on run-down houses, shrouded Arabs pass Hasidim in their broad-brimmed hats and long side-curls. But equally, without a second's warning, something may draw opposites like these mysteriously together until they form an inimitably complex unity—an elusive affirmation of the reality and life that have always been Jerusalem's.

Mysterious and incongruous in the older part of town where traffic has little place, a parked car drowses, protectively sheeted against dust and heat.

His head swathed in the age-old protection of the kaffiyeh, an Arab takes his afternoon ease on the municipal grass of a well-kept park in the new city.

A beggar woman huddles against a wall on the broad steps leading down to the Damascus Gate.

Robed in rich brocade, a priest of the Armenian Church is prepared for mass by an unseen acolyte before the Tomb of the Virgin.

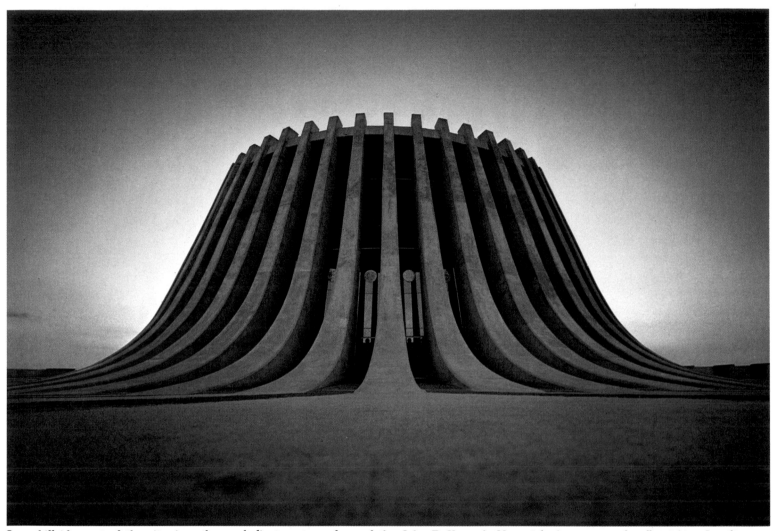

On a hillside west of the city rises the symbolic tree-stump form of the John F. Kennedy Memorial, the gesture of a flourishing Israeli state.

A tall windmill in the Jewish quarter of Yemin Moshe marks the first tentative Jewish attempts, dating from 1860, to settle outside the city walls.

Under Jerusalem's walls two men, identified by their dress as Jew and Arab, casually reduce to human terms the gulf between their peoples.

# Bibliography

**Bagatti, P. B., Milik, J. T.,** *Gli Scavi del 'Dominus Flevit'.* Publicazioni dello Studium Biblicum Franciscanum, 1958.

**Bahat, Dan,** *Carta's Historical Atlas of Jerusalem.* Carta, Jerusalem, 1973.

**Chesterton, G. K.,** *The New Jerusalem.* Hodder & Stoughton, London, 1920.

**Creswell, K. A. C.,** *Early Muslim Architecture (2 vols.).* Clarendon Press, Oxford, 1932, 1940.

**Crowfoot, J. W.,** *Early Churches in Palestine.* British Academy, 1941.

**Dowling, Archdeacon,** *The Abyssinian Church.* Cope, Fenwick, London, 1910.

**Dowling, Archdeacon,** *The Patriarchate of Jerusalem.* S.P.C.K., London, 1909.

**Edersheim, Alfred,** *The Temple: its ministry and service.* Pickering and Inglis, London, 1958.

**Jeffery, George,** *The Holy Sepulchre.* Cambridge University Press, Cambridge, 1919.

**Join-Lambert, Michael,** *Jerusalem.* Elek Books, London, 1958.

**Josephus, Flavius,** *Complete Works.* Pickering & Inglis, London, 1967.

**Kenyon, Kathleen M.,** *Jerusalem: Excavating 3000 Years of History.* Thames & Hudson, London, 1967.

**Kutcher, Art,** *The New Jerusalem: Planning and Politics.* Thames & Hudson, London, 1973.

**Le Strange, Guy,** *Palestine under the Moslems.* Translated from the works of the medieval Arabian geographers. Palestine Exploration Fund, London, 1890.

**Levertoff, Beatrice,** *Jerusalem in the time of Christ.* National Soc. & S.P.C.K., London, 1945.

**Marie, Aline de Sion, Soeur,** *La Forteresse Antonia à Jerusalem et la question du Pretoire.* Franciscan Press, Jerusalem, 1955.

**Moore, Elinor A.,** *The Ancient Churches of Old Jerusalem.* Constable & Co., London, 1961.

**Morrison, W. D.,** *The Jews under Roman Rule.* T. Fisher Unwin, London, 1885.

**Morton, H. V.,** *In the Steps of the Master.* Methuen & Co., London, 1937.

**Oesterley, W. O. E.,** *The Jews and Judaism during the Greek Period.* S.P.C.K., London, 1941.

**Parkes, James,** *Whose Land?* Penguin Books, 1970.

**Parrot, A.,** *Golgotha et Saint-Sepulchre.* Neuchâtel, 1955.

**Parrot, A.,** *Le Temple de Jerusalem.* Neuchâtel, 1955.

**Perowne, Stewart,** *In Jerusalem and Bethlehem.* Hodder & Stoughton, London, 1964.

**Perowne, Stewart,** *The Life and Times of Herod the Great.* Hodder & Stoughton, London, 1956.

**Richmond, E. T.,** *The Dome of the Rock in Jerusalem.* Clarendon Press, Oxford, 1924.

**Roberts, David,** *Holy Land, Egypt and Nubia.* F. G. Moon, London, 1842.

**Runciman, Steven,** *A History of the Crusades (3 vols.).* Cambridge University Press, Cambridge, 1953-4.

**Shanks, Hershel,** *The City of David. A Guide to Biblical Jerusalem.* Bazak, Israel, 1973.

**Sharon, Arieh,** *Planning Jerusalem.* Weidenfeld & Nicolson, Jerusalem, 1973.

**Simons, J.,** *Jerusalem in the Old Testament.* E. J. Brill, Leiden, 1952.

**Thubron, Colin,** *Jerusalem.* Heinemann, London, 1969.

**Vilnay, Zev,** *Legends of Palestine.* Jewish Publication Soc. of America, 1932.

**Vincent, L.-Hugues,** *Jerusalem Antique.* Librairie Victor Lecoffre, Paris, 1912.

**Vincent, L.-Hugues and Abel, F. M.,** *Jerusalem Nouvelle (4 vols.).* Librairie Victor Lecoffre, Paris, 1914-1926.

**Vincent, L.-Hugues and Steve, P. M. A.,** *Jerusalem de l'Ancien Testament (2 vols.).* Librairie Victor Lecoffre, Paris, 1954-56.

**Vogué, Melchoir de,** *Le Temple de Jerusalem.* Paris, 1864.

**Weingert, Gideon,** *Israel's Presence in East Jerusalem.* Jerusalem, 1973.

**Warren and Wilson, Cpts.,** *The Recovery of Jerusalem.* Richard Bentley & Son, London, 1871.

# Acknowledgements

The author and editors wish to thank the following: Aziz Mousa Bukhari, Jerusalem; Rabbi Sheah Yashuv Cohen, Jerusalem; Charles Dettmer, Thames Ditton, Surrey; Canon E. Every, St. George's Cathedral, Jerusalem; George Hintlian, Armenian Patriarchate, Jerusalem; A. Humber, London; Mrs. Joe Klein, London; Mayor Teddy Kolleck, Jerusalem; J. Langmaid, Wiener Library, London; Dr. Baruch Levine, New York University, New York; Linnel McCurry, London; Dr. Anwar Nusseibi, Jerusalem; Mrs. Rae Sebley, Sussex; Mother Sofia, Russian Orthodox School, Bethany; Anna Pugh, London; Rabbi Dr. Steinsalz, Van Leer Institute, Jerusalem; Reverend R. Stoehr, Jerusalem; Canon John Wilkinson, St. George's College, Jerusalem.

# Index

Colour reproduction by Printing Developments International Ltd., Leeds, England
Filmsetting by C. E. Dawkins (Typesetters) Ltd., London, SE1 1UN.
Printed and bound in Italy (January 1976) by Arnoldo Mondadori, Verona.